The cure for leaving home is a loving home.

In *Do You Know Where Your Children Are?* John Benton presents truthful, realistic counsel on how parents can triumph through the turbulent teen years. In these pages, you'll learn how to help your child as he experiences the intense emotional changes of adolescence. You'll strengthen your family ties by creating a stable, love-filled home where your children feel valued, respected and appreciated — a place no child will want to leave before maturity. John Benton has worked with delinquent children and their families for over twenty years, and he knows why a child will rebel — and even leave home.

Do You Know Where Your Children Are?

Do You Know Where Your Children Are?

JOHN BENTON

Fleming H. Revell Company
Old Tappan, New Jersey

Unless otherwise identified, Scripture quotations are from the King James Version of the Bible.

Scripture quotation identified NIV is from the Holy Bible, New International Version. Copyright © 1973, 1978, 1984 International Bible Society. Used by permission of Zondervan Bible Publishers.

Library of Congress Cataloging-in-Publication Data
Benton, John, date.
   Do you know where your children are? / John Benton.
     p. cm.
   ISBN 0-8007-5360-7
   1. Parenting—Religious aspects—Christianity. 2. Teenagers—
United States. 3. Child rearing—Religious aspects—Christianity.
I. Title.
HQ755.8.B46 1990
649'. 125—dc20   90-8411
                                           CIP

Copyright © 1982, 1990 by John Benton
Published by the Fleming H. Revell Company
Old Tappan, New Jersey 07675
Printed in the United States of America

To Marji, Connie, and Jim,
who made Elsie and me proud parents.
To David, Rick, and Judy, whose marriage into the
family
is making us proud grandparents.

Contents

Do You Know Where Your Children Are?

1

Losing Your Teens

Oh, God, it hurts . . . you've lost your teen and you don't know what to do.

This is one of the most tragic experiences parents can face. How in the world did it ever happen?

Things seemed to start right, and you thought you'd never have problems. Remember the joy you felt when your first child was born?

The years rolled by. Remember the "terrible twos"? Remember all the hard work as your kids got older? At times they were such angels; other times you thought they were possessed by the devil! But you kept working at it.

Then came the teenage years.

That's when disaster strikes. Believe me, anybody who raises teens deserves the Purple Heart, Medal of Honor, and whatever other awards for bravery exist.

During the teen years, many parents feel they have lost the children they once felt so close to. They become strangers living in the same house. Problems include drug and/or alcohol abuse, depression, and noncommu-

nication. In extreme cases, teens can end up as runaways
or suicide victims.

In this chapter I'll help you develop a strategy so you
won't lose your teens. Below are five ways to lose them, but
if you can turn the negatives into positives, you will keep
them.

1. You'll lose them if you don't know their world.   In
a popular television commercial for a major name-brand
cereal, a man is quite concerned about his wife, and he is
talking to his daughter about her.

It seems the wife has had a great burst of energy and is
competing in sports as well as wearing clothes only teenagers would wear. Her husband can't understand how this
could be.

Then his daughter picks up a box of cereal. Could it be
that Mom has eaten this cereal and reverted to being a
teenager?

I'm not saying you have to act like a teenager. You don't
have to wear short skirts, know the latest dance, or use the
newest slang, but you have to understand where your teens
are coming from.

Today life is different. Tomorrow it will be even more
so, and who knows what a year may bring? Do everything
you can to try and understand the world your teens live in.

Music changes. Styles change. You and I both know that
teens often seem to do the most ridiculous things you can
imagine. But it's their world. Try to understand it.

The apostle Paul may not have raised teenagers, but he
was right when he said in 1 Corinthians 9:22, "To the weak
became I as weak, that I might win the weak: I am made all
things to all men, that I might by all means save some."

2. You'll lose them if you lose patience with them.
Your teenagers are going through enormous physical and

emotional changes. They've been thrust into a new world that they don't understand. And they are frustrated.

Later in this book I'm going to deal with what frustration can lead to: suicide. But for now, you've got to have patience. God knows about this problem. Hebrews 10:36 says, "For ye have need of patience. . . ." In fact, it is a fruit of the Spirit which He wants to develop in us (Galatians 5:22).

A Japanese friend gave me a wonderful definition of *patience:* "Patience is peace under pressure."

One of the best recommendations I can give you is to get your teens to read the Book of Proverbs. There are thirty-one chapters there, which neatly fit into a month. Encourage your teens to read the chapter that corresponds to the date.

A word of caution: Before you encourage your sons and daughters to read, you had better start yourself. It isn't going to work if you aren't doing it.

Now remember this: They won't always be teens. Later on you'll laugh about some of the things you went through with your teenagers.

When Elsie, our three children, and I went on vacation, I was all keyed up from the ministry. It usually took me three days to unwind. Traveling down the highway in my stressed-out condition, I would sometimes lose patience with the kids' squabbling. "Cut it out back there!" I would command.

Recently, our children—who are now married and have their own families—told me they would make motions with their fingers, like scissors cutting, in response to my order.

Of course, I couldn't see that while I was driving, but the kids used to giggle. I never knew what the giggling was about until now.

We laugh about it now, but then it was serious business.

Remember, the kids will grow up. You too will have your times of laughing about things that almost kill you now.

3. You'll lose them if you are not cool. I don't even know if the word *cool* is still in, but what I'm trying to tell you is, don't try to be perfect.

Now what do I mean by that?

I know you feel it is important to always show your best side as a parent. But let me tell you, you need to let your young people know the mistakes you've made.

And for goodness' sake, don't ever give them the line, "When I was a kid. . . ." We try to impress our kids by telling them about our own childhood. Things aren't that way anymore, and they can't identify with you walking several miles to school rather than taking the bus, working sixteen hours a day since you were six years old, or whatever.

They want to see the real you. Don't hide it.

I strongly advise that, when you encounter difficulties or experience failure, you have your teens pray for you.

Broken relationships are healed by forgiveness. That's what happened between Jesus and us at Calvary. James said it right in James 5:16: "Confess your faults one to another. . . ."

Now, don't get me wrong. I'm not talking about things only you and God should know. I'm talking about how you lost your temper when someone cut you off while you were driving, or the time you said something unkind about your pastor. You need to ask your teens' forgiveness.

What about the times you got angry in front of your teenagers? You need to drop to your knees before them and have them lay hands on you and pray for you. That will really humble you.

That's what I mean by being cool.

4. You'll lose them if you're not living the Christian life. Hero worship is still in. What greater hero than you?

Holiness is a word teens know little about if they can't see it in our lives. Somehow, we've got to show them.

What is your standard of holiness?

Unfortunately, some people have so many gray areas that our teens have no idea what standard to maintain in their Christian lives.

When I was growing up, women had the worst of it. They couldn't wear makeup, cut their hair short, or even wear slacks. We thought that was holiness.

But it wasn't.

I'm talking about what happens on the inside. You might even ask your teens what is their idea of a real Christian. You may be surprised at their answers.

Rather than thinking a Christian is someone up on a pedestal, they probably would think of someone who is a "forgiven Christian."

The encouraging of wickedness in our society is overwhelming. How do we counteract it?

Begin to share with your teens what the Bible teaches about holiness.

Psalms 146:8 says, "The Lord loveth the righteous."

Matthew 5:6 (paraphrase): "They that hunger and thirst after righteousness shall be filled." Our lives can be full if we have that desire.

First Peter 3:12 states, "The eyes of the Lord are over the righteous. . . ."

Discuss with your teens what it is to live a righteous life. Ask them what they think. It will be a revelation to you.

5. You'll lose them if you don't instill hope for the future. You have probably heard the illustration of a glass containing water. Some people look at it and say it is half-full; others look at it and say it's half-empty. That's what the future is to us.

Some well-meaning people are forecasting disaster: earthquakes, famine, war—you name it. It's coming.

Others recognize that these things could happen, but no matter what, Christ is going to be with us.

That's what you must do.

There is one Scripture I've always appreciated, and it goes like this: "Let the whole earth be filled with his glory" (Psalms 72:19).

Although the first-century Church experienced enormous persecution, they also experienced great joy. They knew Jesus was their future.

Young people today are bombarded with the evidence of a difficult future. Drugs are everywhere. Young people are killing themselves. Materialism is difficult to understand. There is the AIDS epidemic. What next?

You can sit down and think logically about the future and get depressed. Instead, you need to get together with your teens and pray about the future. There *is* hope for them.

Start emphasizing the positive aspects of life and minimizing the negatives. There is so much to live for—and so little time.

If you've lost your teens, do me a favor. Have them read this chapter and ask them what they think. If you haven't lost them but fear you will, have them read it and discuss its contents.

You may be surprised to find that things aren't as bad as you thought.

2

Will Your Children Run Away From Home?

You have probably heard the frightening statistic: Over 1 million children ran away from home last year. One of the tragedies of that statistic is that *many of them will never return!*

Adding to that tragedy is the realization that a million children will run away from home this year, a million next year, a million the year after that, a million the year after that. . . .

Young people of this nation are on the move, and they are bailing out of our homes like mad!

Parents are concerned about their children, and they want to prevent their offspring from becoming part of those ever-growing statistics. Probably because my wife, Elsie, and I operate the Walter Hoving Home—a home for girls, most of whom have run away, at some time, from their own homes—I'm frequently asked what makes children run away.

The answers to that question are complicated and varied. But one big reason is you and me. Parents!

Look at it this way. We've never raised children before,

so we're novices at one of the most complicated jobs in the world. Trying to do something we don't know much about always has the potential of ending in failure. What started off as a soft, cuddly bundle of joy in your arms can end up as a frustrating headache! One of those 1 million runaways could be your child! Perhaps one of your children is already part of that statistic.

Or maybe your children are still small, and you wonder if that dark night will ever come when you look into a bedroom and discover to your utter horror that your child is gone. You need help to avoid that moment.

If your children have already run away, you obviously need some encouragement and reassurance.

But what I really want to stress to all parents at this time is that somewhere, sometime, you could face the problem of a runaway.

Even though the statistics are threatening, I want to reassure you that there is hope. Out of my experience of working with thousands upon thousands of runaways, I want to share some insights God has taught me.

I want you to know that this advice isn't like that from a bachelor friend of mine who wrote a book on how to raise children! Neither is it advice from parents with preschoolers who have yet to evidence any independent thinking and who eagerly do whatever their parents suggest.

Along with the hundreds of girls who have come to us for help, Elsie and I have reared three children of our own—all married now. And believe me, it hasn't been easy.

Our children—Marji, Connie, and Jim—have never really run away. Jim, I guess, came the closest to it. He got mad once because he lost a football game at school. Elsie tried to console him, but her attempts backfired. Jim jumped out a window and took off.

He had some problems though. It had snowed, and he was barefoot. It didn't take long for his feet to grow numb from the cold, and he quickly decided that wherever it was he was headed for, it was too far to go without shoes. So he sheepishly came back. And he stayed.

That was the closest we came to it with our own children. But I know thousands of tragic stories. I have lived some of those stories with the people involved.

Once a pastor of one of the largest churches in the United States called me. When I answered, he shouted frantically into the phone, "John, my daughter has run away from home! What am I going to do now?"

I tried to console him, and I prayed with him. But it didn't take me long to learn what was really bothering him. He was overwhelmed with the problem, but what he really was concerned about was his image. He talked about what he was going to tell his church. He wondered if they would throw him out because he couldn't control his daughter.

The more I talked to him, the sadder I became. That man was more concerned about how people would see him than he was about what was happening to his runaway daughter.

Sad to say, that girl never did return home. She must have sensed how she rated among her father's priorities, so she decided to live elsewhere.

That pastor did leave his church. And that's too bad too. If he had handled the situation differently, perhaps he would still be the pastor of that church—and his daughter would be at home.

Those 1 million girls and boys who run away each year—each one of them represents some kind of a family, including a number of Christian families. It could be your fault that they have run away, and yet it might not be.

Deciding who is to blame, at this point, doesn't change the dismal fact: They're gone!

No matter who is to blame, please don't feel that your world has come to an end—that there's no way out. Statistics are on your side; many, if not most, runaways come back home. And as the years go by, they can become the persons God wants them to be. And you can too.

Raising children is a tough job. Someone has said that by the time you've raised them, you've become a professional child raiser. But by that time it's too late. Much of the experience you have gained is for naught because your children are grown and gone!

Before I wrote each chapter of this book, I spent time in prayer for you. I asked the Lord to use what I have shared to help you and your family. I hope you will read this book prayerfully, asking God to make its principles effective in your life.

I believe God still answers prayer. I believe God still performs miracles in answering prayer. I believe God can take seemingly hopeless situations and turn them completely around for His own glory—and our good.

I have seen that happen time after time.

Will your children run away? Have your children run away? Whatever your answer, I believe God wants to work in your family to do more than you have ever dreamed possible. So trust Him! Work with Him! And praise Him!

After visiting many homes, I have concluded that some parents are raising potential runaways and don't know it. Other concerned parents have asked my help because they knew something was wrong.

How about you? Are you raising a potential runaway? Here are four danger signals to look for.

First, Your Children Are No Longer Talking to You

I know that "communications gap" is a worn-out term. But it isn't a worn-out concept. It's very real in many homes. Some children feel that communication with their parents is next to impossible. And some parents have all but given up trying to get anything across to their children. They are worlds apart.

But that kind of situation is intolerable and inexcusable. Somehow we have to span that gap to reestablish communication. And parents are going to have to take the first step. Here are four suggestions to help you span that gap.

1. Love your children. Now that's an obvious recommendation—right? But think about this: Way down deep, do you really love your children? If you don't, you have a serious problem that requires immediate attention.

This is an age in which many parents really don't love their children. In a way, I can understand that. Their children have made it difficult for them. They have run away, taken drugs, stolen, embarrassed them in the community, and generally made life unpleasant. You name it; the kids have done it.

Some parents don't want to have to worry about their children any longer. They are frustrated, worried, hurt, feel like failures, and are out of patience. They tend to blame all their problems on their children and are living for the day when the kids are gone and they can have a little peace and quiet.

Maybe something has happened between you and your children, something very serious. The first thing for you to do is to ask the Lord to restore that love you once had for them. You don't hesitate to ask Him to help you love other people who aggravate you. Why shouldn't you ask Him to help you to love your children?

If you really want to begin to span that communications gap, you can do it readily by demonstrating love. Sincere love may be the only thing that will get across the barriers that have built up between you and your children.

2. Get involved in their activities. *What?* I can hear you protesting. *You mean I've got to go out and play ball with them? Don't you know I'm too old for kid stuff?*

Of course I understand that, and that's not what I'm talking about. Obviously some parents are far better able to get involved in physical activities than others. By involvement I mean the attitude that we all must develop about our children's activities.

If your children are interested in attending sports activities, by all means, offer to take them. Simply taking them and picking them up after the game is showing interest in their activities. And it probably wouldn't hurt you to join them at the game either.

Now don't tell me you don't have enough time. Who does? But have you noticed how we always seem to find time for the activities we enjoy doing? Take time to get involved in what your children are doing. If you don't spend time with them now, you are going to be forced to spend time with them later on when they do things that will *demand* your attention and time.

When they come back from such an activity, ask them how it went. Did their team win? Whom do they play next week? Are they likely to win that game? Ask them how the ice skating went. Did they meet any new friends?

Not only will questions like these show your sincere interest, but there is another amazing benefit. If they know that when they get home you're going to ask them about how things went, they'll try harder to do the right things! If they have been up to no good, it will be difficult for them to lie to you without your being aware of it. Furthermore, they will want to do right because they will be talking to you about it when they get home.

Sometimes when you pick your children up after an activity, why not stop at McDonald's. If you can't afford a Big Mac, go for a Little Mac. But the happy atmosphere of stopping for refreshments together will tell them you like to be involved in what interests them. And the casual, informal atmosphere—where they're doing something they enjoy doing and you're doing it with them—increases the chances that they will use it as an opportunity to talk to you about something that has been troubling them.

Involvement is especially important when boys get into sports. This provides common ground between fathers and sons. So, father, take your son out to a sporting event—and out for a snack afterward.

What if your son doesn't like sports? Find out what his interests are. Forget about your interests and zero in on his! He needs to know you think his hobby, his interests, are worthwhile too and that you're proud of him. So by all means be supportive of his activities. Don't force yours on him.

A favorite pastime for most children is watching TV. Have you really discussed with them some of the things they are watching—or shouldn't be watching?

Now you've probably discussed them all right—but did your discussing become arguing? Was it all one-sided? I'm not talking about that kind of discussion.

TV can become a means of spanning the communications gap, instead of widening it. Find out what types of programs your children enjoy watching. Scan the TV listings for similar upcoming programs. Then plan to watch those programs with them.

Be careful how you handle a situation where they are watching programs that aren't the best for them. If you can objectively view some of those programs with them, you will have a basis for discussing how those programs may be harming them. Then you can steer them away from the bad and toward the good. I think that if parents would sit down with their children to watch certain programs, the children wouldn't watch those programs again. They would be too embarrassed by the content to watch them with their parents there!

A good way, then, to maintain control of the TV is to sit down and watch with your children. If they're ashamed of what they've been watching, they will either leave the room or turn to another channel. That will give you an opportunity to discuss moral values—or lack of them—in certain TV programs.

3. Don't smother your children. Sometimes children stop talking to us because we overpower them. We are constantly "on their backs" about one thing or another.

You need to give your children a little breathing room. When they have friends over, do you have to sit there with them the whole time, while they're talking to their friends? Give them the privilege of space—of being by themselves some of the time.

And be careful when they get home. Don't always greet them with, "And where have you been this time?" I'm not saying you should close your eyes; after all, your children may have been in the wrong place. But watch how you handle that situation. You can do it without giving them the third degree every time.

4. Talk to them about the problem of communication. It seems strange to me that some parents will allow a condition to exist without ever really discussing it with their children. Do your children know you really want to communicate with them? Are they aware that you are interested in their reasons for the lack of communication? If you talk to them about it, you may be amazed to learn why your children have stopped communicating with you.

It happened to me. My son, Jim, seemed to have grown cold toward me. I just couldn't figure it out. Honestly, I didn't know I had done anything wrong. I certainly was interested in his activities. And I certainly love him and try to show it. I didn't think I was smothering him. But somehow communication had been cut off. I had to find out why.

One day when Jim was in his bedroom, I went in to talk to him. He was lying on the bed, and when he saw me enter, he stared straight up at the ceiling. His actions yelled out, "I don't want to talk about it!" But I wasn't going to settle for that.

"Jim," I said, "what's the matter? Is it something I've done wrong?"

He gave me the classic answer: "Dad, there's nothing wrong."

He kept staring at the ceiling, and I knew his response was a cover-up. Maybe he didn't want to admit there was a problem; maybe he simply didn't want to tell me what it was.

I pressed further. "Jim, I just feel that something is wrong between us. Could you help me out and tell me about it?"

Silence. Deathly silence. But I knew this was the time to keep my mouth shut and wait.

Finally Jim turned toward me. I saw two big tears trickle down his cheeks. My thoughts raced wildly. He must have gotten himself into some serious trouble and just couldn't bring himself to tell me.

Then he blurted out, "Dad, a few nights ago I was deeply hurt by the way you were treating Mom."

I couldn't believe it! It had seemed to me like a simple

little argument—even though I guess I had raised my voice to Elsie. But I had no idea it had affected Jim.

I remembered now, vividly, that when I raised my voice, Jim was seated at the kitchen table. I figured he was concentrating on something else. But apparently whatever I had said had really upset him.

God had already taught me the necessity—and the benefits—of asking for forgiveness. A big lump formed in my throat as I looked straight at Jim and said, "Son, will you please forgive me for the way I acted toward your mother the other evening? I'm sorry."

"That's OK, Dad," he answered. "I forgive you."

By this time tears were flowing down my cheeks too. I learned an important lesson from that experience—to be careful what you say in front of your children. Especially when it involves their mother!

I threw my arms around Jim and hugged him; he hugged me back. The ice had melted in our relationship; the barrier had been broken; the communications gap had been spanned. We were reconciled. And it sure felt good.

Is there a communication gap between you and your children? Why not test those four ways of spanning that gap and bringing profitable, healthy communication back into your lives.

Now, here's another danger signal of a potential runaway.

Second, Your Children Are Associating With the Wrong Kind of People

Ever take a close look at whom your children pal around with? I'll deal more directly with that in another chapter. But, at this point, you need to recognize the wrong kind of friends as a potential danger signal.

If your children's friends don't look right and don't act right, you've got a problem. Your children are probably just like their friends!

Now I know it's easy for us to blame other children for being a bad influence on our children. But sometimes our children may be the bad influence on others too! Too often we parents think our own offspring can do no wrong. But they do tend to gravitate toward like individuals. So the kind of friends your children are running with may give some indication of what your children are really like.

What do you do if your children run with the wrong pack? It's a real problem; but here are some suggestions to try to get them out from under the wrong influences.

1. Make sure they go to a Christian camp every summer. This usually works well because it changes behavior patterns. Of all the activities for young people, I would say that attending a good, solid Christian camp or retreat is more beneficial than any other.

When young people go to camp, they are immediately surrounded by Christian kids. If there is a good campmeeting speaker, everybody wants to get on the bandwagon and follow his suggestions. Peer pressure is enormous; the thing to do in camp is to go along with the crowd. But this time the crowd is a Christian crowd acting in a Christian way. At camp young people get saved, filled with God's Holy Spirit, and learn to identify with the good kids—because being good is the "in" thing at camp.

There are some great church camps around for young boys and girls and for teenagers. Ask your pastor about those your denomination provides. Some independent organizations also have "on fire" camps with exciting sports programs and enthusiastic speakers. Even the music is excellent—and appeals to youth. In this atmosphere children are exposed to the Gospel, and God gets a chance to work in their lives.

Elsie and I sent our children to camp. I know it helped them. My friends have sent their children to camp. I've observed that it has helped them. I believe it will help yours too.

Of course, going to camp isn't cheap. Wouldn't it be nice if there were no charge for this great service? But it costs a lot of money to operate a camp. For one thing, camps must comply with a number of state and federal regulations. And you know that the cost of food hasn't been going down lately. Most camp directors have problems trying to meet their budgets, so they have to charge enough to at least recover their operating costs.

Don't let costs stand in your way. Maybe you'll have to do without something else so your children can go. Maybe it will be something as simple as saving a little money each week during the year so that your children can go to camp next summer. But camp is a worthwhile investment. It will be a real winner for them—and for you too.

Some churches have "scholarships" for children whose families can't afford to send them to camp. If the money for camp is absolutely beyond your means, don't be embarrassed to ask your church leaders about what help may be available.

2. Plan activities for your children to counteract the "Saturday night syndrome." Saturday night is still the big night with young people. It's the night to go out. At school they talk about "getting blasted" on Saturday night. They talk about staying out all night.

Young people's activities at the church can sometimes be planned to counteract this. Or you can invite a group of young people to your home on Saturday night. Or take them to a professional sports activity on Saturday night.

Another great idea is to open your home to the young people as a gathering place after a sports activity at school, whether or not it's on Saturday night. Some young people have the idea that the thing to do after a sports event is to go out and drink. Of course, I don't agree with that, and I know you don't either. So invite them over to your house for a party. There, you'll have some control over what happens.

One forward-looking church I know of has a party for its youth at the church after every major high school sports event. It works just fine. I was even invited to speak to their group once, and the kids were really enthusiastic.

I know a little of what goes on after sports activities. I was captain of our high school football team. After every game there is a natural tendency to want to go out and celebrate—but to celebrate in the wrong way. I just wish my church had had special activities for us when I was a teenager. I probably would have gone to church rather than going out and doing things I shouldn't have done.

3. Be firm about whom your children go with. Sometimes it is necessary to sit down with your children and explain to them what kind of people they should select as their friends. If your children have selected someone you don't approve of, then tell them the reasons you don't approve. Of course, you will have to use great discretion— and have valid reasons. In the process of telling your children whom they can't go with, be positive and suggest other people they can go with. Then offer to take them and that friend to an activity together.

Breaking so-called friendships is difficult both for the

children and the parents. Yet there are some that have to be broken. Ask God to give you wisdom in dealing with this problem.

Third, Your Children Are Threatening to Quit School

Some parents think the public school system is all out of whack. There may be some problems in it. But there is one thing that has always remained the same: Many young people don't like to go to school.

Remember your school days? I sure remember mine. And I don't ever remember jumping out of bed early in the morning and yelling, "Yippee! I get to go to school today!"

If you're like me, you lived for Saturdays and vacations.

Schools do have their problems. And not too many children really enjoy applying themselves to their studies. But if your children are threatening to quit school, you have a problem on your hands. How can you overcome that by making school interesting enough for them to stick it out?

1. When they get home, ask them how things went at school. Here again, what you are trying to do is to show an interest in their activities. They'll probably tell you that school was lousy. Ask them why. That becomes a wonderful opportunity not only to span that communications gap, but to provide an opportunity to offer some constructive suggestions about the value of a good education.

2. Encourage them to participate in worthwhile school activities. Most schools have clubs that are good and sports programs that are tremendous. Get your children involved in these activities.

When I was growing up, I think there were only two reasons I went to school: sports and girls. I don't know if it's the same with your children, but it was the activities—not the schoolwork—that kept me going to school.

Involvement works wonders.

3. Help them with their studies. I never could understand the new math. History I despise, and English I never could keep straight. But I'd at least check in with my children to see if there was anything I could do to help them. You can do that too.

When they groan and complain about how difficult it is, groan along with them. If they say the subject is awful, tell them it's like medicine. It tastes terrible, but it's good for them; the best thing to do is to swallow it as quickly as possible.

Hang in there to keep your children in school. Those who quit school end up with too much time on their hands and are likely to get into trouble. That's also when they start thinking about taking off. School can help you through the crisis periods when young people tend to run away.

The final danger signal has to do with Christian values.

Fourth, Your Children Evidence a Lack of Spiritual Values

I have never met a Christian runaway, a Christian drug addict, a Christian alcoholic, or a Christian shoplifter. The combinations are simply incompatible.

When young people have given their hearts and lives to Jesus and have learned to live for Him, they will stay home and ride out the storm. God teaches them that.

The best answer to the runaway problem is for young people to live for Jesus. If your children have grown cold toward God, or if they have never turned their lives over to Him, or if their Christian commitment is only in their heads, you have potential runaways on your hands.

But if your children are spiritually alive, on fire for God, you should be able to sleep well. They will still be home when you get up in the morning.

What can you do to help your children develop these life-changing spiritual values?

1. Expose them to Christ-centered activities.   Church is important because it provides us with an opportunity to expose our children to Christ-centered activities.

By all means, take your children to the youth services at church. Don't leave it up to them to get there on their own. Let them know you're always available to take them if they need transportation.

Don't ever punish your children by telling them they can't go to those youth services. When I was a pastor, I knew of people who did that. I think that's a mistake. Never, under any circumstances, deny your children the opportunity to be exposed to Christ-centered activities.

Thank God for the Jesus festivals that have sprung up around the country. They feature appealing speakers and musicians who can really identify with young people. My children were always helped by attending those activities.

If an evangelistic crusade comes to your church or community, take your children with you. Some evangelists really know how to get through to young people. And God's Word, He promised, will not return unto Him void!

Other activities include: Christian concerts where musicians not only sing but also give their testimonies; Christian films which have powerful messages and visuals that make lasting impressions on youth; even fund-raising activities for church and missions projects.

As you pray and ask the Holy Spirit about these activities, He will open your eyes to the many good things that are available. And as your children participate, they won't have too much free time to get involved in anything else.

2. Be a Christian example for them to follow. I can almost hear you say it: "I'm no angel." I know that. Neither am I. But our young people must have Christian examples to follow. And as parents we ought to be the best examples they could have. Maybe you're protesting, "But I'm such a failure." Perhaps. I know I am. But being a Christian example doesn't mean we live like angels. God has those in heaven.

Being a Christian example means living the Christian life to the best of your ability. When you fall, pick yourself up. When you sin, ask forgiveness. When you do something wrong, say that you're sorry.

All the while your children are watching you. If they see you fall and get up, they will know that when they fall, they can get up too—because you got up. That's being a Christian example.

3. Teach them to have devotions. Family devotions bring the family together for a time of reading the Bible and prayer. But what happens when your children grow up and go off to college or are out on their own? Have you taught them how to have personal devotions?

To do this you will have to start by having devotions together. But then begin to teach them, when they get up in the morning, or before they go to bed at night, or both times, or some other time in between, to spend some time with God, praying and reading His Word. Then when they leave home, they'll be prepared to continue what has become for them a way of life. And they can be assured that God will be with them at all times.

4. Have a weekly family-night discussion. It can be so helpful if you give your children an opportunity to express themselves about the things that bother them.

During our family-night discussion we read a portion of the Scripture and pray together. We have asked our children at times to "preach" at family night. They really enjoyed that—a chance to be the preacher.

In a later chapter I'll talk about a "blind-spot session"—an opportunity for family members to talk about the weaknesses that other family members may have but may not be aware of. Those provide another opportunity for interaction during your weekly family night.

If you establish such a night and make time for it regularly, I think you'll find that the benefits greatly outweigh any sacrifices involved.

Conclusion

I hope you will keep alert for the four danger signals of a potential runaway:

1. Your children are no longer talking to you.
2. They are associating with the wrong crowd—and are probably like the people they are associating with.
3. They are threatening to quit school.
4. They lack spiritual values.

Remember that the Lord can help you overcome each of these danger signals. As you sacrifice and work to help your children, you will have a wonderful experience: They won't become runaways! Or if your child has run away and come back home, then you can share the insights of this chapter with him or her.

I know these observations will help you. I have prayed

that something good will happen in your family. Here's a Bible verse that has been a great source of strength to me. Perhaps it will help you too: "Therefore . . . be ye stedfast, unmoveable, always abounding in the work of the Lord, forasmuch as ye know that your labour is not in vain in the Lord" (1 Corinthians 15:58).

3

What to Do if Your Children Run Away

Having a child run away from home is one of the worst experiences you can ever have. Do everything you can to avoid it.

But if it does happen, here is some advice I have shared with many parents who were undergoing that crisis in their family. It may help you.

First, Don't Panic

I know how it must feel when it happens. You find a note, or a bed that hasn't been slept in all night, or your child just fails to come home after school. You've seen the danger signals building, and now it's happened.

Your first reaction may be that your world has come to an end. Many parents feel that way.

When what has happened begins to sink in, you will probably start blaming yourself. You feel guilty. Or depressed. Maybe you are even tempted to think that you're such a failure you might as well end it all.

All kinds of questions flood your mind. What will your

relatives think? They may have already let you know in subtle—and not-so-subtle—ways that they think you're making mistakes in the way you raise your child. What will the pastor and members of your church think? What about friends and neighbors? How can you face them?

It's no wonder that a lot of parents think their world has come abruptly to an end.

But they're wrong. The statistics are on your side. Even though a million teenagers run away every year, yours probably will return—if you don't panic.

I want you to look at the situation coolly and logically— not from your emotional involvement in it. Think a little about what teenagers face when they run away.

First, it's really tough out there. They opted for the idea of being independent, but they have no idea what that really means. Depending on where they go, they probably will wind up with no food, no shelter, no bed, no friends.

They'll be scared. They begin to realize all the things that can go wrong, that people might try to take advantage of them in some way.

And something strange begins to happen to those run-aways, even those who come to the Walter Hoving Home for help. Suddenly home doesn't seem all that bad. They start mentally building up their parents. And as they get a new perspective on the situation, the problem doesn't seem so big after all. They are like the boy in the parable Jesus told. He left home, but in the far country he eventually "came to himself" when he was feeding the pigs, friendless and starved. And he decided to go back home.

I'm absolutely amazed at how the girls who have come to us still love their parents, even though they have run away from home over what they thought were intolerable situations.

Therefore in one sense, running away has some value.

Teenagers discover it's no heaven out there on their own. They visualize freedom as the greatest, but some of them will probably encounter the wrong kind of people. That may well scare them to death, and they most likely will come running back to the security of your home—never to run away again.

It's like going to jail for the first time. Some of our girls strongly suggest that when teenagers do wrong, the best punishment may be to make them stay overnight in jail! That scares the living daylights out of them. They'll think twice the next time before they do something that might land them in jail again. But unfortunately we too often just give them a little slap on the wrist and tell them not to do that again. But they do it again and again, knowing full well that we'll protect them. So maybe running away, getting picked up by the police, and having to spend a night in jail does have some good points. At least you will want to inform law enforcement agencies that your child is missing. After all, he or she might have been the victim of foul play and really not have run away.

But let's assume your child has run away and discovered that it's no picnic out there in the jungle. The child doesn't come home—he calls home. It's a way of saving face. (It's always a little embarrassing to admit you've made a mistake; children aren't as mature as adults about that.)

The phone rings; you answer, and it's your child. Now what do you do?

You've been on pins and needles all this time, alternating between worry and anger. First, you may worry about some catastrophe having befallen the one you love. In the next minute you're thinking, *How could he possibly do this to me?*

So when you answer the phone, you may be boiling mad. You may feel like lashing out in anger. But bite your tongue. Sit down and take a deep breath—because this is the most critical point.

I have known parents who have blown the whole thing when the phone call came. They have screamed at their kids; they have made unbelievable threats. All that does is to fortify in the child's mind that he made the right decision in running away.

I know I've mentioned the possible value of jails. But by all means don't threaten that you're going to have them thrown into jail. Don't threaten that you're going to beat them when they get home. Think about it: Would you come home if someone told you that?

In a cool, calm, collected way tell them you have missed them and would like for them to come home. Make no demands on them at this point. Attach no conditions. Your object is simply to get them home. After they're home, you can talk intelligently and rationally with them. I'll discuss that in another chapter.

If you blow your cool when they call, you've made it impossible for them to save face, and you'll drive them deeper into the jungle. If you threaten them, they certainly won't agree to come home to restrictions they consider unreasonable. They'll hang up, and you may never hear from them again—ever.

Now it's not my purpose to scare you, but I must remind you that some teenagers will never get back home. I have met some of them. Many of them—both male and female—end up in New York City as prostitutes. Others get involved in serious crimes and are running from the law. Still others are the living dead—hooked on drugs. Others are serving jail sentences. Some of them end up dead at the hands of pimps or perverts.

Where did they all start? They ran away from home. So when they call you, you want to do everything within your power to get them back to the safety of your home.

Here is some practical advice on what to do when they make the first contact with you after they have run away.

1. Pray before they call. I'm sure you've prayed that they will come back. That's good. But there is another prayer you need to be praying. You need to ask God to prepare your heart so that you can be a channel of His love and forgiveness in that initial contact. Build yourself up spiritually for it; then you will be at your best when they call.

I'm assuming that you're a Christian and evidence the fruit of the Spirit in your life, listed in Galatians 5:22, 23, as "love, joy, peace, longsuffering, gentleness, goodness, faith, meekness, temperance [self-control]."

This is the time to put all that to work!

2. Don't blame the child. Have you come flying out of your chair at that suggestion? Just hold steady. I know it probably was the child's fault. But at this point, who is to blame is not of major importance. Our priority is that we want them back in the home. We want them away from the pimps, away from the perverts, away from the pushers. We want them home.

It will be too easy, when they call, to lay all the blame on them. But at this point don't ask them why they did it. That comes later. Don't put the blame on you; don't put the blame on them; don't blame anybody.

3. Ask for another chance. Instead of making them get down on their knees and beg for the privilege of coming home, you take the initiative. Say, "Honey, something has gone wrong between us. Could you please come back and give me another chance to be the mother [father] to you that God wants me to be?"

Then wait for an answer. If there is no response, repeat

the question. Do all you can to get a commitment out of them.

Remember, they may still be full of bitterness and rebellion, and they'll try to bargain with you. If they make demands at this point, simply say, "When you get home, let's sit down like a real father [mother] and son [daughter] and discuss this intelligently." Then add, "I'm sure we can work something out."

I have heard hundreds of stories from our girls about their running away. They all say that this conversation is so crucial. The fact that your child has called indicates that he or she wants some kind of reconciliation, that there is still a spark alive. What you need to do at this point is to bite your tongue and wait until later to get into any negotiating sessions.

4. Set a time to come back.   If they're at a phone booth across town, tell them to wait there—you'll come and pick them up right away. If they're across the country, tell them you'll send them a ticket. Set a definite time and place for them to come back.

Maybe you're horrified at the idea of spending money to get them home. You don't know how you can afford to do it. Maybe you're even thinking that you don't really care whether they come back or not. What then?

I feel sorry for you. And yet I can sympathize. You have probably had it. And you've concluded that you and they might be better off without each other.

You're not alone in those feelings. I have talked to many mothers and fathers who felt that way. They are sick and tired of the hassle and they want that child out of their lives.

But you can't get off the hook that easily. Let me remind you that the Bible says, "Children are an heritage of the Lord . . ." (Psalms 127:3).

Your children belong to God. He has given them to you as a trust, but they still belong to Him. That means you had better do your best to raise them in the fear and admonition of the Lord. God will mark us if we try to cut our children off—if we try to get them out of our lives. After all, they're His.

So I hope you don't feel that you want out. Most parents really do want their children back. They've invested too much time and effort and love to have it all wasted.

I hope and pray with you that after that initial contact, your child will come home. Then you're ready for the second thing, and this is a toughie.

Second, Ask the Reason for Running Away

But be ready. It may well be because of something you've said or done. Let me illustrate.

Many years ago when I was serving as an assistant pastor of a church in Seattle, Washington, I was driving up Beacon Hill. There was a traffic light at each corner, and it seemed that I had to stop at each one.

At one of those lights I noticed a young man hitchhiking. I motioned him into the car, and he ran over and jumped in. As we headed for the next light, I glanced over and noticed that he seemed extremely nervous. Had I picked up a fugitive?

He was visibly trembling, so I asked, "What's the matter?"

"I'm running away from home."

Without even thinking, I responded, "Don't do that."

"I can't help it," he told me.

"Why?"

"My father," he responded.

As soon as he said that, I realized he was probably running from a beating. But he didn't give me a chance to respond as he blurted out, "My old man is an alcoholic. Every night when he comes home, he beats me up. He just came home. And he beats up my old lady. Sir, I just can't stand it anymore."

I was looking for a quick answer. I hadn't had experience with runaways then. So without thinking of the implications, I told him, "Listen, let me do something for you. Let's go to the police and try to solve this."

Well, that was the wrong thing. When I stopped for the next light, he jumped out and took off down the street.

As quickly as I could, I wheeled to the curb and started after him, calling for him to come back. But I couldn't find him.

I never did see that young man again. But I learned a great lesson. There are legitimate reasons teenagers run away.

Thinking about it later, I realized I couldn't blame that young man for running away. Suppose it were me. Could I help it if my father were an alcoholic? Could I take it if he beat me every night when he came home? How long could I stand to see him beat my mother? How long would I stay under those intolerable conditions? I'd probably have run away long before that boy did!

Oh, I know you're not an alcoholic, and you don't beat your kids. At least I hope not. But, still, our children often feel they have legitimate gripes against us. They feel their parents are at fault, and since they can't change the situation, they have no choice but to run away.

I know their reasons for running away are often unfounded and extremely immature. Sometimes the kids are simply not in tune with reality. So our responsibility is to get them to see things as they really are, not as they imagine them to be.

After they are back home, sit down with them and ask, "Why did you run away?"

You may have to ask this several times to get away from a noncommittal answer. They may hate to tell you their reasons. But when they finally do, brace yourself. Undoubtedly they are really going to let you have it with both barrels. That shouldn't surprise you. Obviously they didn't run away because of what *they* did. They'll find some way to put the blame squarely on you.

Hear them out. Don't interrupt. Don't argue. To put it bluntly, this is the time to keep your mouth shut!

While they are letting it all hang out, you sit there and listen. Even though you're boiling inside, you sit there and listen. And listen sympathetically, trying to put yourself in their place. Don't spend the time thinking of what you are going to say in rebuttal. Really listen.

This is extremely important. Parents who develop the ability to let their children express their feelings and ideas have a great advantage. Unfortunately some well-meaning parents have never taken the time to learn this. Whenever their children have said something, the parents have struck back. Sometimes they will tell their children to shut up. Sometimes they hit them. These children aren't stupid. They soon learn not to express their feelings to their parents because they know they will be subjected to a verbal or physical beating if they do.

So you need to learn to let your children have the privilege of telling it like they think it is. If they can express their real feelings without interruptions and threats, you may gain great insights into their behavior. You may even discover the real reasons they have run away.

And the fault for their running away may indeed be yours.

The list of reasons children give for running away is long. Near the top of the list is that mom and dad don't get along.

One time at the Home I received a call from an influential, wealthy man. He wanted to come and talk to me because he was having trouble with his son. The boy kept running away.

I told him to come; I'd be glad to talk to him.

He brought his son with him. I thought it would be best to talk to the father first and get his side of the story. So I had the boy wait outside my office while I talked with his father.

The father was so gracious. He admitted that his business took a lot of his time, but he did try to take time with his son. For instance, he had taken him on a canoeing trip into Canada. They had gone on other similar trips together.

The man just couldn't understand why his son kept running away. And his problem was compounded because the boy had taken a knife and cut himself—not trying to commit suicide, just to mark his body.

I asked if the boy was experimenting with drugs. Sometimes acid and other psychedelics cause young people to do strange things. But, as far as the father knew, the boy wasn't taking drugs.

The more questions I asked, the further I seemed to get from the root of the problem. So I decided to talk to the son.

That was no easy matter. He just grunted his answers. Then I discovered he was interested in Indians. We talked about bows and arrows. I tried to talk a little about Indians. Then I asked him why he had run away from home. He said he didn't know why; he just did it.

I was really at a loss on this one. I couldn't find the answer. I had prayer with the father and son and suggested we meet again. But they never came back.

A month later I heard that the man and his wife had separated and filed for divorce. Then some of the pieces of that puzzle began to fall into place.

Now I'm not saying definitely that the reason that boy cut himself and kept running away was because of his parents' marital problems. But I do know that when parents are having problems in their relationship, it usually shows up in the children. So I suspect this was at least part of the boy's reason for running away. He was aware that his parents were fighting, and he was probably doing these things to gain their attention because he didn't know how to cope with the situation.

Problems between mothers and fathers can affect the rest of the family and cause the children to run away— sometimes because the children feel they are the *cause* of the marital problems.

There are other reasons children run away: improper discipline—too strict or too lenient; not enough love or too much smothering; palling around with the wrong crowd.

Because children frequently feel that their parents are at the root of their problems, you need to learn to let them express their viewpoints. And if you sit there like a concerned parent and listen, you may be able to pick up some clues as to why they really did run away. If you have discovered that in some way it was indeed your fault, you're ready for the next step.

Third, Confess Your Faults and Ask for Prayer

This really works. It knocks down barriers between you and your children quicker than anything else.

I have used it many times and continue to use it. I know I am a person with faults. But God has helped me to use my faults to build bridges of love to those I have offended.

When our older daughter, Marji, was still at home, I got up one Sunday morning and walked out into the living room where she was sitting. As I walked through, she said something. For the life of me I can't remember what she said. All I remember is that whatever she said, I snapped back at her.

I don't know if it was because it was Sunday morning and I was thinking about the message I was going to preach in our chapel service; whatever my reason, I knew I was wrong.

I went down to my basement study to further prepare for the service. As is my custom when I pray, I was walking around. (I walk not merely because I need the exercise, but because if I kneel, I tend to fall asleep. So, many years ago I learned it is better for me to walk and pray.)

I was earnestly seeking God, but it seemed as though the heavens were brass. God seemed a million miles away.

You know how that happens sometimes. You seek God, but you don't hear anything, you don't feel anything. God is silent.

Then this still small voice within me said, "John, go back and apologize to Marji."

I knew who was talking to me.

"God," I replied, "the whole thing was her fault. I feel she shouldn't have said what she did, and she shouldn't have said it like that. She ought to apologize to me."

That ended the conversation. God didn't say anything else. And once again He seemed a million miles away.

I even reminded Him of my problem. "God, I have this message to preach this morning," I told Him. "You have to start talking to me. You know I've got to feel something within my heart before I can share it with the girls."

God kept silent.

I kept pacing, all the while getting more and more frustrated.

Realizing I wasn't getting anywhere in preparation for the service, I finally said, "OK, God, I'll go upstairs and apologize."

Marji was still sitting in the living room. I went up to her and said, "Honey, will you please forgive Daddy for the way he responded to you?"

I was very sincere about it, even though I did feel somewhat stupid. Marji, bless her heart, flashed a big smile and replied, "Sure, Daddy, I forgive you."

"Thanks, honey," I said and headed back to my study.

No sooner had I walked through the door of my study than God said, "Hi, John! Where have you been?"

I tell you, all heaven came down on my soul! Walking almost became leaping because God's presence was so real. I had obeyed His voice, and now He was blessing me.

A little later someone knocked on the office door. There stood Marji, tears streaming down her cheeks. She ran toward me, threw her arms around me, and cried, "Oh, Daddy, I sure do love you!"

My heart broke. Great big tears brimmed in my eyes. I felt such a warmth flowing between my daughter and me. Words can never adequately describe it.

That's what I mean when I say that I have discovered an amazing method of building a bridge of love back to the hearts of your children: Confess your faults to them.

Many other times when I have been wrong, I have remembered this truth. As I have asked my children to forgive me, they have not only forgiven me, but they have also become closer to me.

Other times when I have asked my children to pray for me, they have laid their hands on me and prayed. I know it's humbling. Many times I really didn't want to do it. But every time I have done it, I have had positive results.

Even though our children are all married, Elsie and I are still supported by their effective prayers.

The same thing can happen to you. That child you thought was an unmitigated monster can turn out to be God's angel, being very supportive of you and helping you to grow too.

Conclusion

If your children do run away, remember not to panic. They will probably call home. You need to be spiritually prepared for that call, and the whole focus of it ought to be to get them back home—away from the pimps and the perverts and the pushers.

After they come back, ask the reason they ran away. Be prepared for the fact that they will probably lay the blame on you.

Be ready to confess your faults to your children and ask for their forgiveness. I've found it works wonders. I believe you will too.

I believe this is the plan of God for you and your wayward child. Try it. It's something that works wonders—and gets the healing process started.

4

How to Keep Your Teens From Using Alcohol

What is America's number-one drug? If you said heroin, you're wrong. If you guessed rock cocaine or marijuana, you're still wrong. America's number-one drug is alcohol.

At this point, maybe you are thinking, *My teen isn't a runaway, but I do feel as if I'm losing him. I know he drinks with his friends, but when I confront him, it means another argument and more door-slamming.*

Alcohol is so deceptive. I think Proverbs 20:1 says it best: "Wine is a mocker and beer a brawler; whoever is led astray by them is not wise" (NIV). Some translations say "deceived" instead of "led astray." And that's exactly what is happening.

The next time you watch television, notice how many beer commercials there are during sporting events. This is tragic. Athletes who excel rarely drink alcoholic beverages. Why? Because it would affect their ability. Yet today we are deceived by this seemingly harmless drug.

One of the more surprising things in our ministry happens when Elsie and I visit women in jail. More and more, we're seeing nice-looking young ladies who seem so out of place in prison. Most have never been in jail before. They have no tattoos or scars. They are not hardened criminals. But they are there. The reason? Driving under the influence of alcohol. The sight of those beautiful young women behind bars is horrifying!

In our study of alcohol and teenagers, we discovered that alcohol seems to satisfy certain needs. You see, young people feel good when they drink. But the price of that feeling is high.

As someone has said, alcoholism starts with the first drink. You and I must do our best to stop teenagers from drinking!

Here are some suggestions that will help.

1. Take them to a Skid Row mission. This will accomplish a number of things.

First of all, teens will have the opportunity to see what happens to people who took that first drink. Those dirty, foul-smelling individuals weren't always that way. Most of tnem were decent people, but now alcohol has ruined their lives. Young people need to take a look at what is happening there.

A visit to Skid Row will also give young people an opportunity to see the miracle-working power of Christ. Many mission workers were once alcoholics, and they give their testimonies of Christ's saving power. Your sons and daughters need to know there is hope, even if the problem of alcoholism is a devastating one.

There is always the possibility that your young person may get a real burden for those who are less fortunate. When I started in the ministry years ago, my father used to take me down to Skid Row. I had the opportunity to preach and to see some of those alcoholics come to know Christ. It was a great experience that has stayed with me to this day.

2. Don't drink yourself.   This may come as a surprise, but we have a growing menace on our hands. More and more churchpeople think it is possible to drink and still maintain a Christian life. I have yet to find what I would call an outstanding Christian who is a social drinker. I have found some social drinkers who call themselves Christians, but I wonder about their walk with the Lord.

You may feel that you can handle your alcoholic consumption. Maybe that's true. But if your son or daughter knows you take a drink even once in a while, he or she may try the same thing. Unfortunately, for your child it may become a habit. And then you've got an alcoholic on your hands.

3. Don't have liquor in the house.   I was visiting a minister's home, and I went to his kitchen to throw away my chewing gum. I thought maybe the trash can would be under the sink, but when I opened the cabinet door, I made a discovery. Way back in the corner were some liquor bottles.

Later someone told me about this minister. On occasion he entertained guests who liked to have a cocktail. Though the minister did not drink, he felt it was important to be able to entertain his guests.

What he didn't know was that, as his children grew up, they would soon discover where the booze was. While their parents were gone, they would start taking drinks. I know this is true, as some of the girls in our program have told us they started drinking from their parents' own supply.

Don't ever, and I mean *ever*, have alcoholic beverages in the house. You may make your own excuses for the social drinker, but he can have a deadly impact upon your children.

You certainly don't put poison within your children's reach. Why put alcohol there?

4. Ask the Holy Spirit to show you about the problems of drinking. I travel quite extensively, and Elsie and I have been in Europe a number of times for ministry and vacation. Over there it is culturally acceptable, even for Christians, to have a drink at times. I accept that.

But European Christians have told us about some of the American missionaries who supposedly became part of their culture and started drinking. Some of those missionaries became alcoholics!

What was the difference? As one person explained to me, the nationals might have one drink, but the Americans take two. That's where it starts.

What you and I need to do is ask the Holy Spirit to show us what our limits are. I know mine. I cannot drink because the Holy Spirit has told me not to. What about you?

We have to understand the problem of temptation. When Jesus was confronted by the devil in the wilderness, bread wasn't the real temptation. The question was, who would He obey? Jesus did not make the stones into bread because He wouldn't do what the devil wanted Him to do.

People can argue about drinking, movies, television, or whatever, but the real question is, "What does the Holy Spirit say about this activity for me?" It is important to set a standard of holiness. Ask the Holy Spirit what you should do concerning this issue. Be very honest with yourself and with God, and let your standards be dictated by the Holy Spirit.

5. Talk about it! In another chapter, I will talk about drugs. Though alcohol certainly is a drug, I have treated it separately. But I must repeat my recommendation from that chapter: Talk about it.

Ask your children about the temptation to drink. Are they being approached about it at school? How are they handling it?

Then ask them what advice they would give you on how to handle the problem as their parent.

Now work toward solutions. Ask them what they feel the solution is—and listen intently. Give them the opportunity to express themselves. As you listen, you may be able to detect a struggle they are going through.

One of my favorite stories concerning the problem of alcohol concerns our son, Jim.

Years ago, when we first started in this ministry, Jim was only five years old. I once took him along on a ministry trip, and while we were having breakfast he took a sip of his orange juice and declared, "This tastes just like beer."

I stared at Jim. This little redheaded child of mine was telling me something I didn't want to hear! He had tasted beer and I didn't know it.

"Jim, where did you taste beer?" I asked.

He looked up at me and smiled. "At the neighbor's apartment."

Then he explained to me what had happened. While playing on a Brooklyn street, he had gone to the apartment of one of his playmates. The little guy opened the refrigerator, and his parents had beer there. (Remember, I told you to get it out of the house.) The little boy gave Jim some beer and Jim drank it. I don't think he came home drunk, but he had his first taste at the age of five.

That gave me a wonderful opportunity to explain to Jim about beer. He seemed to understand what I was talking about. Though he had to confront it more than once during his teenage years, I want to tell you where Jim is now: he and his wife, Judy, are the directors of the Teen Challenge of the Ozarks program in Missouri.

Conclusion

You may be dealing with an alcoholic teenage daughter or son. I'm praying with you that, as you face this problem, your teenager will be able to work through it and become the person God wants him to be.

Here are my five suggestions again:

1. Take your teenager to a Skid Row mission.
2. Don't drink yourself.
3. Don't have liquor in the house.
4. Ask the Holy Spirit to show you about the problems of drinking.
5. Talk about it!

5

Will Your Children Become Drug Addicts?

Before some of you shout back at me, "No!" you need to be aware of what's happening in the real world.

Drug addiction is everywhere. When Elsie and I began our ministry, drugs were only in the big cities. Now they are in the suburbs and rural areas. They are probably in your block.

I don't know how many times I've heard these words: "I had no idea my son [daughter] was on drugs."

The reason is, we parents didn't face the drug problem when we were young. It's a new world—a very violent world—and drugs are taking their toll.

In this chapter I want to share with you three critically important ways to make sure your child doesn't become a drug addict.

1. Talk about the drug problem. Who will win the battle over drugs?

You will!

I suppose I've caught you by surprise, but *you* are the key person God can use in your home to keep your children free of drugs.

Here's the way to do it: Talk about the drug problem. If there is a drug bust in your community, discuss that with your children. The story is probably going around in school, but you need to get in on the conversation.

Does your school have a drug education program? Try to find out what is being taught, and learn all you can.

If there is anything concerning drugs going on at your place of employment, discuss that with your children. As I'm writing this book, drug testing has become a very controversial issue. Discuss that with your children. Do they believe people who work in high-security areas should be tested for drugs? How about government workers?

Here's one that will get their attention: Should schoolteachers be tested for drugs?

You might even ask your teens, "How can we stop drugs from getting into America?"

If drug abuse is one of the topics you discuss at home, you will not only get an education for yourself but you will also position yourself with your children as a person sincerely concerned about their struggles with the drug issue.

You may not be a professional on the subject, but at least you can be aware of the challenges your children are facing. God can use you to help them win the battle over drugs.

2. Start the day with affirmations. Now you may ask, "What in the world does this have to do with drugs?" I'll tell you.

Children who are affirmed at home build a very strong self-image. When confronted with drugs, they can say no.

Elsie and I have worked for almost twenty-five years with girls who have been addicted to drugs. We have learned a lot.

As we looked at the failures of these young women, we

found that all of them had basically the same serious problem: poor self-image.

One of our girls, who is a committed Christian today, was told by her pimp, "You're nothing but a filthy, dirty whore!" Sandra told me, "And I believed him."

That horrible self-image led Sandra into many years of drug addiction—and doing *anything* to support her habit. But today she is an outstanding Christian with a very strong self-image.

That may be an extreme case as far as you are concerned. Hopefully your daughter will never become a prostitute, but the basic principle still applies.

Let me illustrate this point.

At our girls' home, the girls have the responsibility of cooking breakfast. Occasionally we end up with burned toast.

But what an opportunity!

I usually hold up the piece of toast and say, "This is the best burned toast I've seen in all my life. How did you do it?"

The young lady who is the morning cook just stands there with her mouth open. She expected someone to yell at her because she burned the toast. Isn't that what usually happens in most homes?

I even take the burned toast to someone else and tell them how excited I am to see such great burned toast.

You get the point.

That morning the girl didn't decide to burn the toast. She forgot it was in the toaster and didn't take it out soon enough.

I could have publicly humiliated this young lady by screaming about the toast. She would never have wanted to put a slice of bread in the toaster again!

But if I affirm her for the burned toast, it's no big deal.

The following morning she will cook the toast again. And I'm sure this time it won't be burned.

We affirm the girls in another way. After the meal, all of us around the dining room table shout, "Let's hear it for the cook!"

We all clap, and some hoot and holler. I wish you could see the smile light up the face of the young lady who just cooked the meal. She is so excited by the public affirmation, she wants to go into the kitchen and cook another meal immediately!

Do you practice affirmation in your home? Let me tell you from my experience, you'll get results when you begin to affirm your children for the things they do.

There's a new philosophy of management going around in business circles. It's called, "Catch them doing something right."

There's a lot of truth to it. Sometimes we play the role of detective too much. We're always looking for our kids to be doing something wrong. When was the last time you caught your child doing something right?

I want to challenge you. Three different times tomorrow, catch your children doing something right and tell them so. Then wait for the response. I know you are going to be surprised.

3. Make a covenant with your children. This covenant is not only for your children but for you as well.

First of all, tell your children you will help them through any temptation to take drugs. They can count on you. You'll do everything in your power to help them through this critical time. In other words, let them know you are always there, available to them.

Have you heard of the management theories called Theory X and Theory Y? They have to do with the management of people in relation to how you treat them, and they work with children. Let me explain.

Theory X says people are stupid. The only way they can be motivated is through fear. "If you don't do this, you're fired," is a good example of Theory X management.

Theory Y says people really want to do a good job. They want to be motivated; they want to be successful. They are very sincere people who need someone to help them.

At one point in your child's life, you probably had a Theory Y relationship. You may have slipped to Theory X lately. As soon as possible, get back to Theory Y. Deep inside, children really want to do good. They want to stay off drugs. They're not stupid—they know the consequences of drug addiction. They see the sordid details of what happens to people on drugs.

Fear tactics don't work! Treating your children as less than human doesn't work, either. Be supportive of them. Have faith in them. Realize they have great potential.

Now here is how the covenant must work.

Your children's covenant with you is that, when they are tempted by drugs, they will come to you and tell you about it. And it's sure to happen.

It can happen at their school. Someone is sure to offer them drugs there. Or just down the street . . . at a pizza parlor . . . at the video arcade.

No matter where or when it happens, they agree to discuss it with you when they are confronted by drugs.

Use wisdom in how you respond. That should be discussed in your covenant.

If your child does not want to make a covenant with you concerning drugs, you may have a serious problem. He or she could be having struggles now. Try to find out.

Times are tough—and they're going to get tougher.

Some of us parents wonder whether or not we should have brought our children into this life. But they are here now, and what are we going to do about it?

Conclusion

After many years of helping troubled young women as well as raising my own three children, I can honestly say that what I have shared with you in this chapter has worked. Though the problem of drug addiction seems to get worse, these principles will work for you and your children:

1. Talk about the drug problem.
2. Start the day with affirmations.
3 Make a covenant with your children.

6

Depression in Teenagers

Depression is often hard to pinpoint in teenagers because they normally go through mood swings during these difficult years anyway, one day feeling on top of the world and the next feeling about as important as a bug. The main clue to depression, however, is that it lasts far longer than normal mood swings do.

There are many possible causes of depression in teenagers, including the following.

Physical causes: Many teenagers go through a period when they don't take care of their bodies. This does not always mean drug and alcohol abuse, but they eat what they want, when they want; they sleep irregularly or not at all; they ignore the mental stress they put themselves under through poor study habits. Parents' pleas for healthy routines fall on deaf ears. The simple fact is, a tired body and mind provide a fertile field for depression.

Individuals with metabolic problems such as diabetes and thyroid disease are also more prone to depression than others, as are those suffering from a long illness.

Proper medication may help the depression in these cases.

Guilt: A person who is carrying an abnormally heavy burden of guilt is prone to depression, whether the guilt is true guilt for past actions or false guilt for imagined wrongs. Teenagers have very active consciences, often assuming responsibility for things that are totally beyond their control. They may blame themselves for the breakup of their parents' marriage, their feelings of betrayal over the death of a grandparent, or some other event.

Anger: When anger is held in, it often turns to self-hatred, which appears in the form of depression. Relationships are vital to teenagers, but relationships often cause anger that the teen is unable or afraid to express, and unexpressed anger can lead to depression.

External stress: The world is an extremely stressful place to live, and teenagers are not very good at handling stress. They take everything to heart, from dying seals to the ozone layer to the lack of support for recycling. When they see very little progress being made, they may give up hope and fall into despair.

Internal stress: Internal stress is basically centered on the way the individual reacts to others he meets. People who suffer from this type of stress *expect* to be rejected by others. This leads them to treat others badly, which in turn brings the rejection they expected all along. It's a vicious cycle. A person who expects to be disliked is a prime candidate for depression.

Another stressful situation is a move from one location to another. This usually means changing schools and making new friends.

Parents should be alert to the symptoms of depression in their teens because depression is a major cause of teenage suicide. Keep an eye out for the following symptoms of teenage depression:

1. Radical changes in appearance. Most depressed teenagers *look* sad and dejected. Nothing seems to make them smile. They might also begin to neglect their appearance. Boys may refuse to shower or shave, and girls may suddenly stop worrying about their hair and makeup. On the other hand, a normally pensive teenager may suddenly begin to act too cheerful and happy in an attempt to cover up or deny feelings of depression. Any sudden change in appearance that lasts for more than a few days should be watched.

2. Withdrawal. Most depressed teenagers feel worthless and hopeless. To combat these feelings, they withdraw and lose all motivation. Favorite activities are dropped, schoolwork suffers, social life ends. All the depressed teen wants to do is sit alone and mope, completely absorbed in his or her own worthlessness. Some of this goes on with perfectly normal teenagers. It is only when parents feel a child is withdrawing for an abnormally long time that they should be concerned.

3. Sleep and bodily changes. A depressed teenager may suddenly begin to wake up very early in the morning, complaining that he can't sleep. He might also sleep much more than usual or have trouble falling asleep. His appetite may change, resulting in a sudden weight loss or gain, and he might complain of headaches, stomachaches, or other illnesses.

4. Emotional changes. A depressed teenager may show many emotional changes beyond the normal ones that come with adolescence. He or she may be anxious or agitated, unable to sit still or concentrate on anything, and even suffer from periodic panic attacks. There may be unusual signs of irritability or aggressiveness. A sudden interest in death and disasters may be evident. Again, it is the continued appearance of these symptoms that should be noted. One good shove of a usually tolerated younger brother isn't cause for concern, but a radical change in behavior might be.

It's not easy for a professional to diagnose depression, let alone a parent. Its causes are often complex and hard to find. But most parents know their children well enough to know when something is drastically wrong, and it would be foolish to ignore the appearance of more than one of the above signs of depression.

If you feel your teenager is suffering from depression, consider taking the following steps:

1. Talk about it.   Find out if there is a specific problem bothering your child, or even a combination of problems. Some depressions are perfectly normal, caused by the death of a friend or relative, the breakup of a family, difficulty with a boyfriend or girlfriend, a failure in school. Grief is not mental illness, and with your support and understanding, in time it will pass. Truly depressed teens cannot pinpoint their problem. They just "feel sad all the time" and have no hope of ever feeling any better.

Do not downplay your child's feelings or tell him or her to snap out of it. Whether or not the cause of the depression seems serious to you, it is serious to your teen and should be acknowledged as such.

2. Build self-esteem.   A depressed teenager has very little self-esteem. He feels everything he does is totally wrong and stupid and he cannot succeed in anything. You know this is illogical, and you need to act on that knowledge. Take every opportunity to encourage and build up your child's self-esteem, pointing out strengths and helping the child build on them.

3. Get him out of the house. Activities and friendships are commonly prescribed ways of combating depression. This will not be easy, since the depressed teenager wants to retreat and be alone, but he needs to come out of himself and interact with others to overcome the depression. Make time for family activities the teen has always enjoyed; encourage friends to drop by and talk. Your success will vary, but don't give up. Continue to sensitively guide the depressed teen toward involvement with others and you will lessen the length of the depression.

4. Take him to a doctor. There are several physical conditions that can cause depression, and you will want to rule them out from the beginning. Take your teen to the family doctor for a complete physical. Your physician can also provide you with references to mental-health specialists if he or she feels this is necessary and will advise your child on proper eating and sleeping habits that will help alleviate the depression.

5. Instill hope. Depressed teenagers have absolutely no hope, despite the fact that depressions generally go away by themselves within six months. At the time, they firmly believe nothing will ever change and they are doomed to a useless existence.

This is where Christians have an advantage, because they know there is always hope through Jesus Christ. Since the sinner has been forgiven, guilt (a common symptom of depression) is unnecessary. The believing Christian has self-confidence, self-worth, and happiness. He knows that "all things work together for good to them that love God . . ." (Romans 8:28). Remind your child of this, or ask your pastor for help. It is true that the Christian may have to learn to patiently wait for these blessings, but they are going to come, and they give hope for the future—something all teenagers need these days.

Conclusion

Once again, here are some steps you can take to help your child overcome depression:

1. Talk about it.
2. Build self-esteem.
3. Get him out of the house.
4. Take him to a doctor.
5. Instill hope.

7

Preventing Teen Suicide

Suicide statistics show that most victims are between the ages of seventeen and nineteen. Why do young people commit suicide when they have their whole lives ahead of them?

One of the basic causes of suicide is frustration. Kids are frustrated about their past, present, and future.

Here are some things that really frustrate teenagers:

1. They feel pressure to be successful. Our society places pressure on all of us to be successful. No one loves a failure.

Our teenagers receive their SAT scores. The scores are discussed among them, and nobody wants to look bad. Because they feel frustration over their inability to handle schoolwork, some teenagers think the answer is to kill themselves.

2. They are frustrated because we are judged by what we get, not what we give. We live in an "I want" society, not an "I'll give" society. The accumulation of material goods is frustrating to teenagers—especially to those who come from lower-income homes.

I fear this attitude has crept into our churches. Material success is equated with spirituality, and this becomes confusing to our teens.

Materialism becomes an obsession. Better cars, better clothes, and better homes—these goals are confusing to a teen who tries to understand the simple life-style Jesus taught.

3. There is a letdown after school.   School can be very intense, especially senior year, when students are trying to "cram it all in." After school is out, there is a lot of unscheduled time for teenagers to deal with. Boredom becomes an obstacle almost impossible to overcome.

4. They have an unknown future.   Teenagers have a way of changing what they want to be, almost on a weekly basis. The reason is that it's difficult for them to decide. Today job opportunities are so varied. Years ago, when I was growing up, kids talked about being firemen, policemen, or doctors. Not today! You name it, and you can probably become one. That's why it is difficult for teenagers to decide who they really want to be and what they should be doing.

5. Teenagers are frustrated because they can't break bad habits.   Recently a young woman who had been in and out of our rehabilitation program left for the last time. She had come to us several times but never stayed long enough to get her life straightened out. That was her way of dealing with her frustrations. As soon as she encountered something difficult, she would leave.

This last time she left, the young woman was picked up by the police. In a jail cell, she took her blouse and hung herself.

When we heard, we were devastated. But we knew this girl's frustration at not being able to break her drug habit.

Teens face not only habits of drug addiction but other frustrations ... overweight, promiscuity, pornography, smoking, bulimia, anorexia ... and the list goes on.

Now let me share with you how you can help your teens get rid of some of these frustrations and prevent the tragedy of suicide:

1. Define success. There are so many definitions of success, but the one I like the best is, "Success is discovering God's will for your life."

This has to do with the talents God has given us. Jesus talked about the person with five talents, the one with two talents, and the one who had only one talent. When they were used successfully, there were great rewards. When they weren't used, there was punishment (Matthew 25:14–30).

Sit down with your teens and pray with them concerning the talents God has given them. Then help them discover what they should be doing in life.

Success has also been defined as a journey. I like that, too. It is not a destination, and our teens ought to know that. Success is never measured by what we have, what we accomplish, or even by how popular we are.

Let your teens know that some of the most successful people in the world are not wealthy or well known, but in the eyes of God, they are very successful because they have fulfilled God's will for their lives.

2. Begin to teach your teenagers what the Bible says: "It is more blessed to give than to receive" (Acts 20:35). By all means, set the example. Are you a giving person? If not, you had better forget about trying to teach your teenagers and start with yourself. Like it or not, we teach by example.

Giving means sharing time as well as money. Set the

example of looking for opportunities to give. That might mean inviting someone who needs a meal to supper. Maybe it means running an errand. Encourage your teens to open their hearts to someone in need. Then work with them to satisfy that need.

Don't let the doldrums set in after your son and daughter get out of high school. Begin to plan activities during their senior year, before they get out of school.

Help your teen line up a job. If you can, take some of your vacation in the spring so you can help him or her plan for that summer job.

Possibly he can work in a church camp or, if there is a transition time between high school and college, he may want to volunteer at some charitable organization.

3. Don't let the future be unknown. Begin teaching your children to put their trust in God. We should always be making plans for the future. Become filled with a sense of expectancy—believe God for the miraculous. Don't be afraid of the future! Challenge it with your faith in God, and allow your teenagers the privilege of exercising faith with you.

The future can be exciting if you start to plan it that way.

4. The best way to break a bad habit is to replace it with a good habit. My desire to get up early and pray for at least an hour every morning taught me a great lesson about developing good habits.

I am not an early-morning person, so it was going to be doubly hard to do this. But I knew it had to be done if I was to be effective in ministry.

Replacing a bad habit with a good one sounds simple, doesn't it? But at first it was very difficult.

There were three keys I learned: desire, discipline, and delight.

First came the desire. I really felt I should pray that hour—I desired it.

The next step was probably the hardest. There was the discipline of getting up earlier and having that time alone with God. I needed to face the realities of the day after having spent that time with God. I had to force myself, and I mean literally force myself, to get up. But I knew I had to do this. And I did it.

The beautiful part is, I now spend an hour and a half or longer with the Lord each morning. Because I made this great discovery . . . I have delight!

As I write, I have embarked on another weight-loss program. The doctors said I have to get down to 176 pounds. I had found the key, and I went through the process again. My *desire* was 176 pounds. Then I *disciplined* myself to eat the right kinds of nutritious food. And, to my *delight,* I've lost 10 pounds.

Here's what I want you to do: Have your teenagers read this chapter. Then tell them you'd like to discuss it with them.

This will be a wonderful opportunity for a meaningful discussion with them about the terrible problem of suicide. Be sure to ask how they feel about what you are discussing. And *listen.*

You could be surprised or shocked at the response you get. But be honest and open, and hopefully your teenagers will never consider suicide.

Conclusion

In review, here are the steps to go over with your teens:

1. Define success.
2. Begin to teach your teenagers what the Bible says: "It is more blessed to give than to receive."

3. Don't let the future be unknown. Begin teaching your children to put their trust in God.
4. The best way to break a bad habit is to replace it with a good habit.

8

How to Make Your Home Like Heaven, Not Hell

Trudy was one of the girls who came to us for help. She was born and raised in Texas. Her father had a very good income, and she apparently had all the necessities of life.

But Trudy had a real battle: She was overweight. She became extremely conscious of her problem, and it seemed to her that every day her folks were "on her case" about her weight. Of course, that only made matters worse, and she would run to her one comfort: food.

The situation at home became intolerable. One day Trudy had had it—I mean, she really had it. So she took off. At that particular time the hippie movement was in full swing, and Trudy thought there was only one logical place to go: San Francisco.

She hitchhiked all the way. Because she was so overweight, I'm sure not too many men made passes at her, so she arrived safely. And in San Francisco there was one area to go to: Haight-Ashbury.

When she got there, the short, overweight girl from Texas really didn't know what to do or where to go. But it didn't take long for that to change.

A bearded long-hair walked up and asked, "Hey, baby, what ya doin'?"

Trudy, still a novice in the ways of the world, blurted out, "I've just run away from my home in Texas."

"Hey, baby, no problem, no problem," the young man replied. "Come to my pad. I'll be glad to share what I've got."

Trudy knew down deep that the hippie was up to no good. But where could she go? What reason could she give him for not going? To her anything was better than going back home. So rather hesitantly she followed the hippie to his pad. It was filthy, with few furnishings except for a mattress on the floor. But it was a place to stay. And although Trudy was used to much finer things in life, she moved in. It was, after all, the only offer of help that she had had.

It didn't take long for her to learn that the young hippie was also a drug addict. And it didn't take long for him to encourage her to get high. After all, that took her mind off her problems and her surroundings.

Before long Trudy was also addicted.

But there was no money for drugs. There was only one answer to that. Trudy had to hit the streets as a prostitute.

The whole idea of prostitution was absolutely disgusting and degrading to her. She loathed going to bed with perverted men. But apparently there were plenty of men who wanted a fat woman. She had lots of business. And, as part of a vicious cycle, her drug habit got worse—because she felt the drugs helped her forget the disgusting, degrading things she was having to do.

Thank God, Trudy's story didn't end on the streets of San Francisco. Someone told her about the Walter Hoving Home. Tired of running, she made contact with us, and we accepted her into our program. When Trudy came to us, Christ gloriously saved and changed her.

One day while she was with us, I asked her why she had run away from home. I'll never forget her answer. She looked me straight in the eye and declared, "Brother B, I ran away because my home was hell."

I stared at her. I couldn't believe that a home in Texas, with all the niceties of life, could possibly be a place to run away from. I wondered how a girl raised in such comfortable, clean surroundings could stomach the filth of a hippie pad. So I said, "Wasn't the Haight-Ashbury section of San Francisco hell also?"

"Well, not at first," she replied. "When I moved in with this guy and met all his friends, never at any time did anybody hassle me about my weight. Not once! In fact, it was just the opposite. Everything was love, love, love. We hippies were going to bring peace to the world. But, of course, the inevitable happened. I started smoking pot to join them in their euphoria. Then I graduated to stronger drugs. Before long I was hooked and ended up as a prostitute to support my drug habit."

"Then why didn't you go back home?" I asked.

"That's just my point, Brother B. If I went back home, I knew it would be hell. I just couldn't go back to that."

She paused, letting it sink in. Then she leaned toward me and asked, "You wouldn't want to go back to hell, would you, Brother B?"

So that's the way some of our teenagers see their homes—as hell. Whether we realize it or not, many forces are working today to destroy the home. And sometimes parents almost inadvertently cooperate with those forces.

I don't know how many times I have warned young people about the hell at Times Square in New York City. But still they run away to it. Why?

Because they're thinking about the hell that's going on inside their homes: the hassles they get; the friction; the arguments; the blaring TV; the lack of love and understanding.

There is no way we can reason with them that it's worse out there. They can't believe that anything could be worse than their own homes.

Now please don't get me wrong. I don't want to find fault with you. But I hope and pray that this chapter will do something to improve your home. If there isn't a change for the better, you have probably already lost the battle.

Let me give you three ways to make your home like heaven, not like hell.

First, Reduce the Noise Level

Have you really opened your ears to the noise level in your home? If you were to take a twenty-four-hour recording, you'd probably be amazed—and horrified—at what goes on in your home. That noise level adds to the confusion and lack of peace. It keeps everyone on edge.

Here are some positive things you can do to reduce the noise level in your home.

1. Talk in a normal tone of voice. Let's start with you. How do you give orders? Are they commands made with a loud voice? Or are they requests made in a spirit of love?

Now before I lose you, let me assure you that I'm right in there with you. I probably commanded more than I requested. But I learned that my commands were less effective than my requests.

Please remember this: Your children will be a reflection of you. If you command in a loud voice, they'll answer back sharply in a loud voice. But if you speak softly, you will find that they will speak softly too.

By all means, never scream. Screaming says you have lost control of your emotions. Tests show that people who scream are not effective in their relationships. So if you want to be effective, give your requests in a normal tone of voice. You'll be amazed at the results.

2. Check the noise level of the TV. I'm not about to take all the joy out of your life by kicking the TV out of your home. I have one. And I admit they have some value. There are a few wonderful programs on TV. Not many, but some.

But with guns blazing, monsters shrieking, and all the rest, the noise can contribute to making your home a part of hell and not heaven. Every thoughtful American knows that TV is getting worse. I am flabbergasted at the profanity, at the violence and sex openly displayed—even encouraged. Our kids are watching—and being affected by it all. So the noise level I'm talking about here is not just in decibels; it's also in the confusing, non-Christian life-styles portrayed.

Another part of the noise level of the TV concerns where you have your set. I hope it's not in the living room.

Have you ever visited a home where tne TV was on? What happens? Everybody sits there glued to the TV. That set kills more conversation than you can imagine. When friends should be together for wholesome conversation, the TV dominates. If someone tries to talk, he gets angry looks. And that's sad.

So by all means get the TV out of the living room. At the time our children were growing up, I put the TV in the basement. It was cooler down there during the winter, and I noticed that watching TV didn't become a central activity in our home.

Put your TV where it won't continually interrupt family life.

And turn it off sometimes. I am amazed at the number of families who turn their TV on in the morning and don't turn it off until they go to bed at night. Whether anyone is watching or not, the set is blaring out its noise all day long. That's bound to have an effect upon the atmosphere of the home. Turn it off and enjoy the peace and quiet.

Second, Play the Right Kind of Music

Elsie and I didn't raise our three children without problems. One of the biggest problems was the music.

I grew up in a traditional church that taught it was wrong to have worldly music in the home. And I tried to pass that on to our children.

But I have been absolutely overwhelmed and frustrated in recent years to see young people with long hair and beards singing gospel songs. The two didn't go together in my book. And worst of all, these hippie-looking, so-called Christians were invading my household with their music! I decided it was time to stand up for righteousness and put a stop to this nonsense. So I tried—and failed.

I don't know how it happened, but our older daughter, Marji, had somehow slipped one of those record albums into our house. I saw the record jacket, and my head bounced off the roof. I was not going to allow that stuff in my house!

I stared at the photo of the recording artists. To me these people were repulsive. They were the antithesis of what I thought good Christians ought to look like. I didn't see how any good thing could come out of their mouths.

I ordered Marji to pull the record off the record player. Bless her heart, she immediately obeyed.

After I had cooled down a little, she brought the record jacket to me and said, "Daddy, you may be interested in the words to that music they were singing."

I guess I'm beginning to show signs of old age. My hearing is going, and some of my hair is falling out. And I tell you, when it came to listening to the words of the music that those people were singing, I couldn't for the life of me figure them out.

But I can still read. As I sat there reading the words on the record jacket, I could hardly believe what was happening. Those lyrics were some of the best words I had ever read in all my life! They showed an amazing understanding of the meaning of the Christian life. But, listening to those noisy records, I couldn't understand the words at all. But my children could.

I tried to approach the situation logically and rationally. Since the words were so inspirational, I asked Marji to put the record back on. This time as the voices sang, I followed the words on the record jacket. Words and music flowed together. Then Marji began to sing along with them.

Suddenly I knew I had been terribly wrong. Those words were providing great spiritual benefit for our children. So the record stayed.

What I had to learn was that there are many kinds of Christian music. Just because I don't happen to care for one kind doesn't make it less "Christian" than the kind I like.

Many types of music can bring inspiration and faith. That's the kind to get. As with many things there's always a middle road that is acceptable. I still don't care for some of the music our Christian youth are playing, but I honestly feel they are being helped by it. Musical tastes differ. It would be wrong for me to impose my preferences in music as the only truly Christian kind.

You may not agree, but will you at least take the time to try to listen to the words that are being sung—or read them, if they're on the record jacket? If you're like me, you're going to have trouble understanding them. But they'll probably surprise you.

Now let's move our thoughts away from Christian music, and let me give you a warning. If worldly music is in your home, you're in trouble. I have heard the testimonies of some rock musicians who became converted. By their own confessions, before they were saved, they were singing about the benefits of taking drugs, engaging in illicit sex, and all the rest.

I believe the worldly music industry today is one of the most deplorable there is. Watch out, Mom and Dad. Don't let that monster invade your home.

Gather your children together and have a discussion about the effects of that kind of music. It has a tendency to be a part of hell, not of heaven. You certainly don't want that in your home.

On the other hand, if you have good gospel music, you will bring a wonderful, peaceful spirit into your home. That spirit, enhanced by God's Spirit, brings security and peace. Your children won't run away from that.

Third, Be Holy

"Are you kidding?" I can almost hear you saying it.

Before I tell you the benefits of being holy, let me give you some Bible verses to show you the necessity of this suggestion.

In 1 Peter 1:16 God says, "Be ye holy, for I am holy." And Hebrews 12:14 encourages us to "follow . . . holiness, without which no man shall see the Lord."

Why holiness?

Every home has an atmosphere, a "spirit" about it. Some are good; some are bad. Some are full of peace and God; others are full of evil.

We have it at our Home. I'm told it is a good spirit, a good atmosphere.

I love to have visitors because many times when they walk in, they tell me they can feel the presence of God. For some of them it is something they are encountering for the first time. These dear people look around in utter amazement; they don't know what is happening.

But I know; other Christians know. They are sensing the presence of the Spirit of God.

Walter Hoving, retired chairman of Tiffany's, whom our Home is named in honor of, has the best explanation of it that I have heard.

A few years ago, because of zoning complications, it seemed apparent that we were going to have to move. We couldn't get permission to put up buildings we needed. We had to have more room. The solution seemed to be to relocate.

I went to Tiffany's to forewarn Mr. Hoving that this might happen. When I told him it might be necessary to sell the Home and move elsewhere, he replied—and I shall never forget his words—"John, we can't do that. Jesus is in those walls up there."

When Mr. Hoving comes to visit us, he experiences it the same way. And I have seen it time and time again. When people come into our Home, they are warmed by the presence of Jesus. It isn't hocus-pocus or magic. But it's a spiritual reality.

Why does this happen?

I really believe it is because of the dedication and commitment of our girls and our staff at the Home. We believe in holiness. We believe in dedication. In prayer. In faith.

In love. We want to be people who are approved of the Lord. And He is with us.

Now don't get me wrong. We're not angels. We still have our feet on the ground. We make mistakes. But in the mistakes we ask for forgiveness from the Lord and from each other.

In spite of our limitations and our weaknesses, we are determined to live lives that are holy. As I say, we do not always succeed. But we're certainly always trying.

And that is the benefit of holiness. When we make an honest effort to be holy, that attitude generates the spirit of Christ in our homes.

I saw this vividly in the homes of the people in my congregation, when I was pastor of a church. Those people who were walking close to God had a wonderful spirit about them. Those who were lukewarm had a different kind of atmosphere. And those who were living in sin had an evil atmosphere about their homes. You could sense it.

As a parent, ask the Lord to help you to be holy. You can't do it in your own righteousness, but you can do it through the righteousness of Christ.

As you personally set your priorities and spend time on your knees in your home, you will discover that God will always be there. As you fully seek the Lord and His will, through that consecration you will create an atmosphere of spiritual power that will bless those who come into your home—including your own children.

Conclusion

You can make your home a part of heaven or a part of hell. The choice is yours. But if you want the atmosphere of heaven there to help you, remember the three suggestions I have shared in this chapter:

1. Reduce the noise level.
2. Play the right kind of music.
3. Be holy.

As you do these things, I believe you will begin to see the difference in your home. Maybe slowly at first, but it will change for the better. Great peace will come to your home, and your children will feel secure and content.

9

You're a Total Failure—What Then?

You will fail as a parent. All parents do it sometime.

Failure comes in all kinds of packages. Some failures seem as though there is no possible recovery. Others are like roller coasters—ups and downs. I've had both kinds.

The first time was with our son, Jim. He and some friends did some damage to the house next door while the people were on vacation. I thought my world had come to an end when my neighbor called the sheriff. Think of how it looked for me. I was the director of a home to help delinquent girls!

When I learned the sad news of Jim's escapade, I hardly knew what to do: kill or love.

The boys had to pay for the damage they had done. Jim worked many hours to earn the money, but he finally paid it off.

But my ego was completely destroyed. And I was so embarrassed over the whole thing. But do you know something? I survived. And I learned that my ego was not the most important thing in a situation when my kids did something wrong.

There have been other times—some so severe that I really can't mention them. Oh, they were tough on me. At the time I thought there was no possible way out. But again, I've survived every one of them. So will you.

Whenever I think of failures that stay around to really nag you, I think of the story of David Wilkerson and his brother Jerry.

David, Don, and Jerry were all raised as preacher's sons. David and Don became leaders of Teen Challenge, a ministry to delinquents, which David founded. In fact, the name David Wilkerson has become synonymous with work among delinquent youth.

But Jerry turned out wrong. He became an alcoholic.

I shall never forget preaching on Saturday nights at the Teen Challenge Center in Brooklyn years ago. Among all those junkies sat Jerry Wilkerson, still an alcoholic. He would listen to the Gospel but never come forward to admit that he was a sinner and needed to get back into a right relationship with Christ.

Then one evening something happened at the Glad Tidings Church in Manhattan. They were filming *The Cross and the Switchblade,* and Pat Boone, who played in the film, was in the city. He and David Wilkerson had a meeting at Glad Tidings, and Jerry came to hear what they had to say.

At the close of the meeting David pointed Jerry out and asked him to come forward and get right with God. It was beyond imagining. And Jerry got up out of his seat, came to the altar, and gave his heart back to Jesus. David sent him to the farm in Pennsylvania where he sent other men and boys who needed to start a new life.

Thank God, Jerry got a satisfying Christian experience. For many years now he's been living as a consistent Christian. But I know all those years when Jerry was living as an alcoholic were a terrible drain on the Wilkerson family.

How it must have nagged at them and embarrassed them. How their hearts must have ached for their wayward brother. Yet the family trusted God, and He answered. Today Jerry is a real man of God.

I, too, have had problems in the family in which I grew up. My father died still praying for the salvation of his oldest daughter, Olive. My sister had been away from God for many years. Her husband, Mike, wasn't a Christian either.

I can still remember the irritation in our home when Mike and Olive came to visit us in those days. It was a little embarrassing for the rest of us to get ready to go to church while Mike and Olive kept making excuses about not going. I know Dad must have often wondered why it had to be this way, especially when he had prayed so hard.

But after my dad died, their son Mike, Jr., found Jesus as his Savior. He invited his parents to church. I don't know what it was that convinced them to go, but they went. God miraculously answered prayer, and Mike and Olive gave their hearts to Jesus too.

I don't know if Christians can look over the portals of heaven and see what's happening on earth. If not, I hope the next person who makes it to heaven tells my dad that his prayers have been answered. Mike and Olive have come "home."

Mike and Olive have become great Christian believers. And I think I am the proudest brother they could have.

So I know that when it comes to raising children, the pathway can easily be strewn with failures. When that happens, we have a few choices: for example, jumping off bridges, burying our heads in the sand, disowning our kids, or running away from home. None of these choices are really solutions. Let me give you six ways to help you overcome failure.

First, Believe the Problem Can Be Solved

What do some people do with failure? The Bible tells about one who did something drastic. Judas Iscariot, after he had betrayed Christ, went out and hanged himself. Believe me, that is not the solution!

But what about you? Suppose you have failed. Now what?

Let me quickly give you the starting point: Believe the problem can be solved.

Don't try to believe for the solution at this point. That comes later. Just believe that through the Lord's intervention—miraculous or otherwise—the problem you have as a failure can be solved. Whether you're the reason for the failure, or someone else is, believe that through this, God will be honored and the problem will be solved.

I have been through some rough, trying times. For example, when we were missionaries in Japan, our son died. I had to take a shovel and dig his grave myself. That was almost more than I could bear. But I survived.

I know what it is to have this ministry to delinquent girls on the verge of bankruptcy. Many times. But God has always supplied the need.

I know what it is to work with people, trying to head them all in the same direction. Yet people continue to pull in opposite ways, and it really tears your heart out. But God has always overcome the problem, and the end has brought peace.

The list goes on. Some things I dare not mention. But there is one thing I can assure you of: Whatever it is, those problems can be solved. Believe that.

If you don't already have one, you ought to buy yourself

a promise box from a Christian bookstore. It's a box with little cards in it, a Bible promise on each card.

I have memorized, and, believe me, I have experienced many of the promises of God. Like Psalms 34:7: "The angel of the Lord encampeth round about them that fear him, and delivereth them." I believe all Christians have angels; their assignment is to deliver us.

Here's another promise: "No weapon that is formed against thee shall prosper; and every tongue that shall rise against thee in judgment thou shalt condemn . . ." (Isaiah 54:17). If I understand that promise right, nothing that is against God's children will prosper.

Here is another beautiful one for protecting help: "For the Lord God is a sun and shield: the Lord will give grace and glory: no good thing will he withhold from them that walk uprightly" (Psalms 84:11).

That list goes on too. There are thousands of promises in God's Word. We can claim them because God's Word can carry us through every adversity.

I heard a story about the Reverend Dwight L. Moody, founder of Moody Bible Institute and Church in Chicago. He was a great man of God. But since he was human like the rest of us, he too had his failures.

Pastor Moody had a custom of visiting his parishioners in the afternoons. About five o'clock he came home for supper. But one night when he came home, Mrs. Moody noticed he seemed depressed. She just didn't know what to do about it.

His depression went on for weeks. Mrs. Moody prayed and asked God for a plan. The Holy Spirit gave her one.

The following day she waited for her husband to come home at five. Sure enough, one look at his face told her that he was still depressed.

When he opened the door and dragged himself in, head

down, she let out a bloodcurdling scream: "God is dead! God is dead!"

She went flying around the room, waving her arms frantically and still screaming, "God is dead! God is dead!"

Moody stood there in shock. He didn't know what to do. It seemed she had lost her mind. So he ran over, grabbed her by the shoulders, and shook her violently, screaming back, "God is *not* dead!"

She stopped immediately, dropped her hands, and looked him right in the eye as she said, "Well, by the way you've been acting the last few weeks, I thought God had died."

I don't know if that really happened, but the story packs a great truth. Sometimes our actions cry out to others that God is dead.

Don't let God die during your failure. You need Him. And you can believe Him. Your problem can be solved. You are going to see the answer!

Second, Don't Fail

Does that shock you? What do I mean by saying, "Don't fail"?

Some people use failure as an excuse. Because they have a low image of themselves, they convince themselves they really are failures. They have no trouble identifying with the Born Loser.

And you know something? You become what you see yourself as. If you believe you're a failure, you fail! But, bless God, if you are what you believe, then begin to believe you will be successful.

God's purpose for us is to succeed. But if we fail, He has a remedy for that.

Remember the Bible story where Jesus and Peter had a confrontation? Peter, very self-assertive, said he was never going to forsake Jesus. Even if everybody else did, Peter declared he would stay true. But Jesus said that before the rooster crowed twice, Peter would deny Him three times.

Jesus was trying to warn Peter not to fail. But Peter insisted on his self-imposed confidence. The pressure got intense when Jesus was arrested and led away. And Peter did deny Jesus three times.

The lesson of that story is that Jesus tried to prevent Peter from failing. If Peter had only asked Jesus more about the upcoming event and what he could do to overcome the problem, he would have been saved from the terrible embarrassment and failure of being one who turned his back on his Lord.

In Joshua 1:8 the Bible says, "thou shalt have good success." I believe God wants us to succeed.

Success, of course, is a lot easier to handle than failure. So determine in all your relationships with your children that you are not going to fail; you are going to succeed.

But if you do fail, consider the third point.

Third, Decide If You Have Really Failed

You called it failure. But was it?

Did you know that the steps of a righteous person are ordered by the Lord? (*See* Psalms 37:23.) When you get some perspective on the situation, what seemed to be a failure may not have been a failure at all—just a stepping-stone to success. You see, God has a different way of evaluating what we call failures and successes. He sees everything from the viewpoint of eternity.

Now I hope you are sitting down when you read this,

because I'm about to tell you something that may knock you off your feet.

Did you know that *it is really impossible for a Christian to fail?*

I know that may sound revolutionary. But here's what I mean.

No matter what happens to us, Jesus is always bigger than that problem. He has the ability to take that apparent failure and use it for His glory and honor. Then it's no longer a failure!

Let me illustrate.

Some friends of ours had a promising son, who was active in the church. Ralph sang in the church quartet and seemingly was well on his way.

But something happened to him in his later teens. He got in with the wrong crowd, quit going to church, and completely got away from his spiritual heritage.

Then Ralph began to steal. The police caught him and reprimanded him since it was his first offense. But he kept it up. When the police caught him again, they put him in jail.

His parents tried to help him. His wrongdoing became an overwhelming problem—a failure, if you please—for that family. They didn't know what to do.

Finally Ralph was sent to prison for stealing. Totally unrepentant, when he went into prison, he bragged that he was going to escape. If they caught him, he said, they'd have to bring him back to prison feet first. In other words, he was saying they'd never take him alive.

While in prison Ralph seemed to have a change of heart. He did well, and they made him a trustee. But the day they made him a trustee, he escaped.

He left Washington and ended up in California. The police followed him and eventually surrounded a hotel where he was staying. They expected him to be armed and dangerous.

Two policemen burst into his room. Ralph was underneath the covers in the bed, and they assumed he was asleep. Just as they edged toward him, Ralph threw back the covers. He had a gun in each hand and came out of that bed with the guns blazing. The two policemen were killed.

Other police finally captured Ralph. At his trial he was found guilty and sentenced to die in the gas chamber.

It was one of the most tragic things that could ever happen to any Christian family and to any church. How could one of their young people go so wrong?

But here's what happened.

After Ralph was incarcerated, he began thinking about the horrible mess he had made of his life—and of the lives he had so pitilessly ended. His father and his pastor visited him, and Ralph got back to God. He apologized to the families of the police officers he had killed.

That, of course, didn't change the facts. Even though he had become a Christian, Ralph still died in the gas chamber. He did make his peace with God before he died, and I believe he went to heaven. The Bible says that the blood of Jesus cleanses from all sin—and that includes murder.

But Ralph's story didn't end in the gas chamber. His father went from church to church, telling about Ralph and the wages of sin.

I was in one of those meetings, and I'll never forget the altar call. Many young people went forward to receive Christ as their Savior. God used that father in an unusual way to reach young people and turn them to God before it was too late.

I've often thought about that situation. That father could have gone into hiding after his son's execution. He could have tried to find solace in privacy. But instead he straightforwardly faced that horrible situation, and God had a way of turning it around. Ralph died; that's true. But because he died, many are living today, having received eternal life in Jesus Christ. And that's no failure.

There are many other similar examples. And here is something else I never quite get over. Because some of our girls had become junkies, prostitutes, and alcoholics, that sin led them to the Savior! Had they not become junkies, they might still be trusting in their own self-righteousness and never have come to Christ. Had they not been sentenced to prison, they might never have come to know the Lord.

Now I must admit that I don't quite understand that. But I do understand this: Christ has the ability and power to take what we call failures, turn them around, and make them blessings.

That's why I say Christians can't fail. No matter what happens to us, Christ is bigger than that happening. He can take that seeming failure and turn it around to His honor—if we learn to trust and believe Him.

Fourth, Get the Right Kind of Advice

Advice can be bought by the truckload. Even more of it will be given free. Ask anybody, and they will give you advice. But not all their answers are right!

Let me give you four sources for getting good advice.

The first is obvious and is the first place you should always go: the Lord.

When our failures in trying to raise our children hit us over the head, the first person to go to is the Lord.

Ask Him to help you. The Bible promises that God has

wisdom for us which He will give us—if we ask Him for it (James 1:5).

The second source is your pastor. God has ordained pastors to care for the church. When you're hurting, take your burden to your pastor. God has used many pastors as His channel of wisdom and understanding during times of crisis.

Moreover, you do need to talk to someone. If you keep the problem bottled up inside you, you may explode. God has given your pastor the ability to lift your burden in prayer, and you will feel much better as you share this burden with him. God can help both of you to come up with the right answer to your problem.

Another excellent source is successful parents. Ask them how they did it. Latch on to their experience. If they've been successful, God has undoubtedly helped them. And you might be surprised at what they tell you. Most parents can hide their failures. All people see are their successes. But if you ask for advice and they level with you, you probably will be surprised to learn how they struggled through problems similar to yours—and eventually came out victorious.

The fourth source of advice is good books. Check your Christian bookstore to find those that can be extremely helpful.

You have four sources of good advice readily available to you. When you receive the right advice, you can make the right decisions.

Fifth, Blame God; They Belong to Him

I suppose the easiest of all these helps is that when our children fail, we can blame God.

You have a right to. The Bible says, "Children are an heritage of the Lord . . ." (Psalms 127:3). That means they really belong to Him. They are His kids. If they fail, that's His problem.

But let's not stop there. God in His infinite wisdom and mercy lends our children to us to care for. So we have a responsibility too.

In the church I grew up in, we dedicate children to the Lord. The dedication service is almost like repeating your marriage vows. The minister asks you if you will raise the child in the fear and admonition of the Lord. And you answer, "I will."

Then he asks if you will lead this child at an early age to know Christ as Savior. Again you answer, "I will."

The point is well-taken, I believe. Since children belong to the Lord, they are loaned to us to care for. We can trust God to help us with His property. Just possess that kind of faith, and you will begin to understand that God is more interested in your child's turning out well than you are. And He wants to help you in your task of raising that child. So follow Him. He is the best Parent.

Sixth, Resist the Temptation to Quit

As I told you before, I know a little about apparent failure. And whenever it happens to me—which seems to be quite often—I have one quick response. I feel like quitting.

When the disciples failed Jesus, He didn't kick them out and start over with new disciples. He stayed with them, tenderly, gently, leading them on. I believe that's exactly how He feels when we fail. He wants us to stay with Him.

Jesus always seemed to be giving special attention to those who failed. Look at how He treated Peter.

There's something about Peter that I can identify with. He was the one who was up one day and down the next. Sometimes he had enough faith to walk on water. Other times he looked at the waves and started to sink. Sometimes he was so full of the glory of God that he could boast that, come what may, he'd always stick with Jesus. And a few minutes later he was running away like a scared jack-rabbit.

That's the way I struggle with my emotions too.

But there is a beautiful story in the Book of Acts about Peter. After Jesus arose from the dead and ascended to heaven, the Early Church was left without a leader. But who served as spokesman in those days? Who preached the sermon on the Day of Pentecost? You're right. Peter.

If I were chosen to serve on the selection committee, Peter would have been at the bottom of my list. Look at the charges I could have hurled at him. He couldn't stand the pressure. He denied Christ. He acted on impulse, not with well-thought-out plans. He just didn't seem to have leadership qualities.

But the Holy Spirit selected him and empowered him to become a great leader. Why? Because he knew how to handle his failures.

What about you? What are you going to do with your failures? Don't be a Judas; be a Peter. Face your failures as Peter did. He took one look at Jesus and knew he had done wrong. In his heart he repented and went out and wept bitterly over his failure. Then the Holy Spirit was able to use him mightily in the Early Church.

You're no different from Peter. You're no different from me. All of us are subject to normal failures. We break under pressure. But Jesus is the One who makes the differences in our lives. He is the One who understands us totally. And He is the One who will lift us up when we fail.

In our ministry Elsie and I see so many failures. Our girls come to us because they are failures. But they leave the Home completely changed. Even after they graduate, they still have some failures. But there is one thing we have tried to teach them, and it really seems to work. It's this:

"Failure is not so much going down; it's not getting up after you are down."

That is so true. We go down, and that may not be so bad. Everyone does. But here is the dividing point. There are some who won't stay down!

If you have failed, I want you to reach out right now to Jesus. He is extending His hand to lift you up. Grab it, and get up. You won't be a failure when He takes your hand.

Conclusion

Let me go over those six key points again:

1. Believe the problem can be solved.
2. Don't fail. Think success.
3. Decide if the experience really was a failure. Does God view it differently?
4. Get the right kind of advice—from God, from your pastor, from successful parents, from good books.
5. Blame God when your children go wrong; after all, they belong to Him. But remember, you share the responsibility with Him.
6. Resist the temptation to quit.

As I sit here writing this book, I feel God's presence in a special way reaching out to help you. I believe the Holy Spirit is going to do something for you.

Just repeat this prayer and mean it:

Lord Jesus, I confess to You that I'm a failure. Forgive me for the way I have failed. I believe now that because You forgive me, my past is clean, and I can look to You in faith. I believe right now that You are going to solve this problem and bring the answer I need. On the inside I stand up. In Christ's name I am overcoming this failure and will see You turn it into a success. Amen.

I believe in you, and so does your Savior and Friend. I know He is going to help you.

10

If Birds of a Feather Flock Together, Whom Are Your Children Flying With?

One of the most distressing and perplexing problems we parents face is trying to get our children to be friends with people we approve of. And that isn't easy!

We tend to believe a myth about those with whom our children associate. For one thing, I know we are defensive about our children. But I think we need to face up to some facts.

Be careful when you tell your children not to go with certain people because they might have a bad influence on them. Of course, that may be true, but most of the time your children will go with the wrong people because *they* are wrong. Birds of a feather do flock together.

If your child is really right, he or she will go with the right kind of people. And if something is not right with your child, he or she will usually link up with those you consider wrong.

I don't know how many times I've heard it: "My child got in with the wrong crowd and turned out bad." That's often a cop-out. The truth of the matter is that your child was probably bad before he or she associated with that crowd. In fact, your child may have set the standard for that wrong crowd. Somebody's child did!

However, I don't want to be harsh or overly critical. Children have minds and personalities of their own. They are not merely extensions of their parents.

I have faced friendship problems in raising our own children. Believe me, I know it's no easy task trying to get them to associate with the right kind of people.

That's why I want to share with you six keys to help your children develop the right kind of friendships.

First, You Make the Earliest Decisions About Their Friends

Later on, of course, they will have the privilege of selecting their friends. But until they earn that right, the decision is up to you. And your decisions can point the way toward their making the right decisions later on.

Already I can hear the outcry of your child when you choose the friends: "But you don't trust me."

I can't tell you how many times I've heard that one. And I still hear it constantly from the girls who enter our program at the Home. But we settled that issue long ago. I have learned that this kind of trust is not a gift to be given whenever we are asked for it; this kind of trust is something you earn.

My first real encounter with this was when our girls' home was still in Brooklyn. Our ministry was in its infancy, and we were trying to develop policy and procedures. Through my inexperience I decided that it would be good policy for us to trust the girls.

It seemed like the right thing to do at the time. There had been some rumblings among the girls that we didn't trust them. They needed a better sense of self-worth, and maybe this would help.

So I gathered all the girls together and announced that we were going to trust them. Whereas before, they were not allowed off the premises for any reason unless a staff member was with them, now we were going to trust them. In the afternoons for an hour they could leave the home if they stayed within a two-block radius. In other words, I was going to trust them for an hour and two blocks.

They all smiled and thought we were absolutely the greatest. Everything seemed to be working well.

If I recall correctly, that policy lasted for two whole days. Then I discovered how my theories were riddled with in-experience.

The day after I made the announcement, one of our girls was typing late in the afternoon. She kept bending over the typewriter, her forehead almost hitting the keys. I saw her and felt sorry for her.

"What's the matter, Carmen?" I asked. "Are you sleepy?"

She slowly raised her head; her eyelids drooped.

"Oh, Brother B," she answered, "I'm so very sleepy. Last night I just couldn't sleep at all. I'm so sorry, but I just can't keep my eyes open."

"Why don't you go take a little nap?" I suggested. "It doesn't look like you're accomplishing much anyway." And I laughed.

She slowly got up, thanked me profusely, and headed toward her room. I felt rather proud of myself for having come to the rescue of a sleepy girl.

It wasn't ten minutes later that a staff member, a former addict, came to me and said, "Brother B, did you know that Carmen is high?"

"Are you kidding?" I replied in surprise. "She just left here a couple of minutes ago to take a nap. She was real sleepy—said she didn't sleep last night."

The former junkie laughed. "Brother B, I can see that you've got a few things to learn. She's higher than a kite."

Should I argue with a former junkie and tell him he was just suspicious? Or should I try to find out what had really happened? I decided on the latter approach.

I ran after Carmen, went into her room, and started to grill her. She insisted she was sleepy, not high.

I didn't know what to do. I had had no experience in working with addicts. I really hadn't seen anyone high before—so I didn't know if what I was seeing was "high" or not.

But the next day the truth came out. Carmen had indeed gotten high. Now she hadn't disobeyed the rules. But within the two-block radius she had made contact with a pusher and bought some drugs.

I realized I had made a terrible mistake. You can't trust people until they have earned your trust. From that moment on, if a girl came in and complained that we didn't trust her, we immediately replied, "Of course we don't!"

Sometimes they are shocked by that abrupt answer. But we go on to explain that trust is something you earn. It is not something that is given automatically on request.

It is the same way with our children. We have every right to keep our eyes and ears open to what goes on. After all, they are children, not small-sized adults. But we must explain to them that trust is something you earn.

It is the same way when you tell them you are going to select their friends. If they start to scream about it, tell them that later on they will be given the privilege of deciding who their friends will be. But be sure to get this point clear, because you are now in a situation that demands sensitivity. If you try to cram certain friends down their throats, they will regurgitate! You can't *demand* that someone be friends with someone else.

I know what I'm talking about. Our Marji started going with a handsome young man who had a fantastic car—but who wasn't a Christian. I don't know if it was the boy or the car that Marji fell for; but with his car and his good looks, I had a real problem.

They started dating. And believe me, my wife and I spent some restless evenings when those two were out.

The more I prayed about it, the more confused I became. Marji was always a good girl. I felt she could be trusted. But this relationship just didn't seem right.

Finally I told Marji that she couldn't see the boy anymore. I felt perplexed and like a failure—and like a mean old ogre. But deep within my heart I now felt that this was what God wanted.

A few days later, when the tenseness of the situation had cooled, I talked with Marji about it. I expected her to respond negatively and was really surprised by her answer. She told me she knew her relationship with this young man wasn't right, but she just couldn't bring herself to make the decision to end it. She thanked me that I had made that decision for her.

I suddenly realized that there are some decisions we have to make for our children until they are mature enough to make those decisions for themselves. Your children may be waiting right now for you to make that kind of decision. On the outside they may rebel. But down deep inside they will be grateful when you step in and help them. So stand up for what is right—and hang in there.

Now let me try another one I almost hesitate to tackle. But it's coming up more and more these days. What would you say if your daughter became close friends with a boy of another race?

One reason I bring that up is that it happened to us. Marji is very attractive, and she became acquainted with a black boy. He liked her, and. . . . Now before you accuse me of prejudice, let me tell you something about my black friends. At the Home we love the black girls as well as the white girls. I know that God is no respecter of persons. And I don't believe we should be either. We simply have no room for racial prejudice.

Furthermore, we have a black girl on our staff. Frannie Wingate is just like the rest of the staff to me. When I look at Frannie, I don't see black. All I see is Frannie.

She has a beautiful daughter named Donna who has been raised at the Home. Our son, Jim, grew up with Donna and treats her like a kid sister.

In fact, all three of our children have grown up in our ministry living among girls of all races. They have no racial prejudices that I know of. To them a girl is a girl. She can be black, white, yellow, blue, green, or pink. Color makes no difference.

Marji, growing up in this environment, couldn't care less about what color a person is. To her, it's the person who counts, not the color. And I'm glad for that, because in the eyes of the Lord everyone is seen as just the same.

But dating presented a special problem, and I think Marji sensed that. One day she sat down and asked me, "Daddy, what would you say if I brought a black boy home, and he was my husband?"

I stared at her. I'm sure my mouth dropped open. I was facing a moment of truth. For years I had carefully taught by word and example that God is no respecter of persons. I had told my children that in God's eyes black and white are the same. But marriage? What was I going to say?

My mind raced wildly. Could I honestly say I had no racial prejudice? Could I throw my arms around that black boy as I would throw my arms around any other son-in-law? Would I be proud of my grandchildren?

I breathed up a quick prayer. I needed an immediate answer, and God gave it to me.

I looked right at Marji and said, "Honey, there's only one thing I could say. I would say to your husband, 'Welcome home, son.' "

Marji stared at me. Then a great big smile brightened her face as she said, "Daddy, I'm glad to hear that. But I want to tell you something. I don't intend to marry a black person."

I didn't know whether to show relief or not. But I do know one thing. If Marji had gone ahead and married a black person, I know I would feel the way I said. It would still, today, be, "Welcome home, son."

Maybe you think I'm absolutely wrong in that kind of attitude. Or maybe you're agreeing with me 100 percent. But let me help you with this in case you confront it in your own family.

I am not advocating racially mixed marriages. However, if it does happen, we dare not judge on the basis of race. If we try to say that blacks are different from whites, we are in deep trouble. There is no difference to God.

But marriage presents special problems in adjustment.

Here's how we explain it at the Home. To me it's no different than if Marji married a man who weighed 500 pounds. Marrying a man that size presents enormous problems. When you and your husband walk down the street, we tell the girls, people will turn and stare. When you fly on an airplane, there are special arrangements that have to be made. When you are at a restaurant, people will be watching—all because your husband is terribly over-weight. That feature attracts attention. And if you don't like to be the object of that kind of attention, then don't get yourself into that kind of situation.

It's like that when a black and a white marry. Such a relationship will attract attention. People will say things, and people will think things.

In a racially mixed marriage the couple has to have great emotional stability to withstand the inevitable criticisms that such a relationship brings. Furthermore, their children will face unbelievable difficulties and adjustments. Are they prepared for that eventuality?

I know a little about being on the receiving end of prejudice. When we lived in Brooklyn, Jim was the only white boy in an all-black school. And he was persecuted because he was white. One day Jim came home—he was only about five years old then—and said, "Mommy, I wish I was black."

I understood something about prejudice.

You may say it's wrong for people to stare and comment about a racially mixed marriage. Perhaps so. But we are not going to change society overnight. The stigma is still there today. With all the other problems and adjustments that marriage brings, the couple will have to be mature enough to take the criticism and ostracism that a racially mixed marriage encounters.

If a couple is prepared to handle all those problems, then I say they should go ahead and get married. Maybe some people can handle it. But it usually doesn't seem to me to be so.

And that brings me back to the point I have been stressing. Because your children are children and lack maturity of adult judgment, you must select the right friends for them at first.

Second, Teach Them to Be Soul Winners

If you train your children to look upon their friends as prospects for the kingdom of God, they will have no problem keeping the right kind of friends. You see, if an acquaintance is up to no good, just a few words of the Gospel will separate that person from your child; that wrong kind of friend won't be able to tolerate someone who is religious. It makes him uncomfortable.

Yet if there is a deep spiritual need in that acquaintance and he or she can be reached by the Gospel, what a beautiful relationship that can be!

God has given us a number of wonderful people on our advisory board at the Home—people like Dale Evans and Pat Boone and other capable people.

One of them is a psychiatrist. Some people are afraid of psychiatrists, but Dr. Quentin Hyder is a man of God we are all proud of.

He and I were once discussing what type of person would best qualify for entrance to our Home. Without a moment's hesitation Dr. Hyder said, "The best person you can get is a potential soul winner."

He's right. Not only do we win a person who has been a junkie or an alcoholic, but we win a person who has great potential.

When you look at your children, see them as having great potential as soul winners. Their soul winning will help them to grow spiritually, and they will also be able to win other people to know Jesus as Savior.

So teach your children to be soul winners. Get them books on how to evangelize. Expose them to witnessing ministries and encourage them to take a course in your church in such ministries. Believe me, if your children become soul winners, you won't have problems with their friends. They will all get converted!

Third, Teach Them to Invite Their Friends to Church

This is one way they can become soul winners. And I have seen this work beautifully. In fact, some of our children's friends have come to know Jesus as their Savior because we encouraged them to invite their friends to the church services we have at the Home.

Encourage your children to do that too. Even offer to pick up their friends if they need transportation. Urge your children to invite their friends to any church-related activity, even to camps. Wherever spiritual activities are taking place, be sure your children feel free to bring their friends with them. Remember, our aim is to win them to Christ if they are not already Christians.

Our son, Jim, played football. That thrilled me because I was captain of my high school football team.

Jim maintained a positive Christian testimony in school and on the football field. They even had him praying before the games—like an unofficial chaplain.

Now his prayers for victory didn't always work. I think they lost more games than they won. But at least people knew where Jim stood.

That's why you need to encourage your children to bring their friends to church. It will let them know that your children have a spiritual standard. And those who

want to know more about the Lord will be attracted to
your children.

Fourth, Make Their Friends Your Friends

Now I am not advocating that you act like a child again.
Or that you smother your children so they don't have the
opportunity to deepen their friendships on their own.

What I am saying is that you need to develop a positive
attitude toward your children's friends. Whether you know
it or not, your children look to you for approval of their
friends. And deep within they will know of your
approval—or disapproval—even if you don't say so. Now
here's a touchy point. If your children's friends meet your
qualifications, but you don't really love them, your children will quickly pick up that spirit. They are sensitive.

I have seen some parents turn their backs on their children's friends. That's not really Christian. And furthermore, it leads to rebellion.

Whenever your child selects friends, take a sincere interest in them. Learn their names, hobbies, interests, what
they like to do. Take a personal interest. As you do, if a
friendship is questionable, you will have an opportunity to
talk intelligently about the relationship. But if you haven't
tried to make them your friends, your ability to discuss
that relationship will be greatly limited.

Whenever Elsie and I have done things with our family,
we have encouraged our children to bring their friends.
That way we have gotten to know their friends, and some
have been saved.

Those children who come from non-Christian homes
really need to know the Lord. Those from broken homes
desperately need adult friendships. Let them be your

friends. God will honor this, and you may be able to reach them for Christ.

Fifth, Pray for Your Children's Friends

I am assuming you have established a time of devotions with your children. As you pray together, remember your children's friends by name.

This will do several things. First, it lets your children know you really do care about their friends.

Second, it will help your children learn how to carry a burden and concern for their friends too. After all, what is a friend? A friend is someone who really cares.

Third, if you are praying for your children's friends and their needs, your children will become more aware of those needs and bring more of them for prayer in your devotional time together. That begins to build a warm relationship between you, your children, and their friends. And let me tell you, relationships are really "where it's at."

Sixth, Buy Them Books About Christian Celebrities

A lot has been said critically about Christian celebrities. I know some well-meaning people think we shouldn't glorify the Christian entertainer or Christian athlete—that they are no better in God's eyes than anyone else. That's partially true.

Since God is no respecter of persons, and since all our righteousness is as filthy rags in His sight, we all fit into the same category. We are all sinners saved by grace.

But that doesn't change a facet of the situation one iota. Our young people are hero worshipers—whether we like it or not.

You may be surprised whom your children "worship." They know the famous singers. And those singers may live rotten lives—using drugs, engaging in ungodly, immoral living. But there is something about a celebrity that draws children.

I'm like you. I don't like it. But that doesn't change the fact that they are hero worshipers.

There's something we can do. We can give our children Christian heroes to admire. And one way we can do that is to give them books about these outstanding Christians.

Be sure to give sons books about Christian athletes. And, thank God, there are many men who have taken natural talents and have excelled. They are tremendous heroes to our children.

Give them books about Christian film celebrities. I know some of these people, and I have found them to be great Christians. I may not always agree with all they do, but there is no question in my mind of their sincerity and sometimes overwhelming faith in God. Young people, being hero worshipers, will listen to the words of these celebrities because they really admire them. So let your children know that heroes and Christians can come out of the same mold. Get their personal Christian testimonies into the hands of your children. This will help counteract the theory that the Christian life is dull and drab. We know that's not true, but children may need an object lesson to help them to understand it.

I believe the Christian life is the greatest thing going. Let your children see its reality in you. But also let them see it through the stories and testimonies of Christian celebrities.

Those people who think the Christian life is tough should talk to our girls at the Home.

All our girls were out in deep sin. You can't imagine the terrible things the devil did to them. When they were junkies, they had no vacations. They worked almost twenty-four hours a day, seven days a week. They were in constant danger. Some of them got cut up by perverts. They had to work hard as sinners. Life was no picnic.

But when they came to Jesus, all that changed. He has given them great peace and love—something they lacked all those years before they met Him.

That's why I don't buy that mistaken notion that the Christian life is tough. Jesus came to give us life—and that more abundantly. It's exciting to live for Him.

We Christians have the greatest thing going—Jesus. In moments of crisis He gives us the grace to ride out the storm. In moments of failure He lifts us up. So be sure to give a positive image of the Christian life to your children.

Conclusion

Well, friend, do you have a little bit of work to do on this one? I am praying that the Holy Spirit will give you great wisdom as you help your children develop the right kind of friendships. This may be hard, but have patience. In the end you will see the beautiful fruit of your labors. Just remember the six keys to better friendships:

1. You make the early decisions about friends.
2. Teach them to be soul winners.
3. Invite their friends to church with them.
4. Make every friend of your children your friend, as you go out of your way to get acquainted with them.
5. Pray for your children's friends, privately and in family devotions.
6. Because children are hero worshipers, get them books about or by Christian celebrities.

And don't forget to teach them about the greatest Friend of all, the One who sticks closer than a brother, the One who has promised never to leave them nor forsake them. Their friendship with the Great Friend will affect all their other friendships too.

11
Building a Bridge Over Troubled Waters

I'm sure you've heard it; it's almost become a cliché: a bridge over troubled waters. Some creative people have capitalized on the popular song and written lyrics that say that Jesus is the Bridge over troubled waters. I like that.

But I want to assure you that there is a way of building a bridge of love back to your children. You don't have to remain isolated from them.

Some parents see their children slowly drifting away from them—like a ship heading away from shore. They wonder when their children will disappear over the horizon, never to be heard from again. And sometimes that happens.

Let me change the metaphor. Think of your children as having drifted away and landed on some island. How can you get to them to make them understand your love?

You want a bridge strong enough that you can go to them and they can come to you.

Unfortunately some parents have given up at this point —because bridge building is a lot of hard work. In fact, just recently a mother called to tell me she didn't want her daughter ever to call home again. As far as the family was concerned, that daughter was dead.

I know of one family that got so upset they actually went to their minister to see if they could have a funeral for their daughter. She was alive and well. She had been a junkie; that didn't bother them too much. But she became a Christian. When she did that, as far as her parents were concerned, she was dead. They didn't want any more to do with her.

Fortunately God had other plans. This beautiful young lady married a handsome young man and had a child. The grandson melted the hearts of the grandparents, and they eventually welcomed their daughter back home. Actually I think they welcomed their grandson, and the daughter came with him!

The gap between you and your children can be bridged if you are willing to take the initiative; *they* probably won't. Here are six ways to build that bridge. The first one is tough; the others are a little easier.

First, Confess Your Faults to Your Children

Sound crazy? Well, if you will think about it and actually do it, I will guarantee that it will work.

One day I received a phone call from a well-known woman. If I mentioned her name, you would probably recognize it. So let's just call her Virginia.

Virginia told me she had just taken in a young teenage girl who lived in the community and had run away from home. She was calling me for advice.

Virginia knew the girl's parents, and that placed her in an extremely difficult position. If she called the parents, the girl would immediately take off to who knows where. But if she didn't contact them, she knew they would be greatly upset with her. In that quandary, she called me.

We made arrangements for her to bring the girl to our Home. We knew that if the girl took off and ended up in New York City, only eternity would reveal what happened to her. I am well acquainted with the Times Square area, and a number of runaways end up there in prostitution and on drugs. Sometimes the parents of these girls don't have a second chance with their daughters. The girls take up with a pimp and before long are found somewhere— dead.

But I knew that if we could keep this girl for a few days, Christ would have time to work in her heart. That would produce a change in her attitude and outlook. Then we could contact her parents.

The girls in our Home have God-given abilities to reach the hardest hearts. They know where these young kids are coming from—after all, they've been there. I knew they stood a good chance of getting the Gospel across to this young runaway.

Virginia brought her up. I must admit I was apprehensive about our taking in this reputed "bad egg." She turned out to be a timid, cute little blonde whom you just wanted to reach out and hug.

I don't think it took more than two days at the Home before she gave her heart to Jesus. Then her eyes sparkled; a smile constantly played across her face. Jesus again made the difference.

Elsie gently shared with her the importance of calling home. She told her that her parents undoubtedly were at wit's end worrying about what had happened to their daughter.

Elsie called them, and they were overjoyed to know their daughter was safe. When we asked if she could spend a few more days with us, they gladly consented.

After those days the girl felt she ought to go home again. She admitted she had made a horrible mistake and wanted to make things right. You can believe that delighted us. After all, that's what our ministry is all about.

Earlier Virginia had told us a little about the girl's family. They were very wealthy. The father was a Wall Street broker.

I looked forward to meeting him. I really wasn't hoping to receive an offering from him! We don't charge the girls who come to the Home; our ministry survives as God directs people to give their freewill offerings. I was looking forward to meeting him because I was hoping to see a beautiful reconciliation. You see, reconciliations are priceless. Money can't buy them. And, thank God, our Lord provides them free!

Well, the girl's father drove to our Home in his expensive automobile. We were waiting out on the porch with the daughter.

The father got out of his car and stood there looking toward his daughter. She looked back, not quite sure what she should do. I held my breath. Was he going to start screaming and yelling at her for running away? Would she yell back, and would that start the whole problem all over again?

The suspense was almost unbearable. The father just stood there staring.

Then all of a sudden the daughter threw her arms out wide and took off toward her dad. When she started running, he started toward her. As they collided, there were arms all over the place. It was so beautiful!

Then they both began to cry. And I started to squall too. There may be times when I think I'm tough, but in a moment like that my heart just melts.

We invited the father in and talked with him. Later as

the daughter went to collect her things, he and I stood alone in the hallway. I shall never forget what he told me.

"Reverend Benton," he said, "this has been one of the most devastating things that has ever happened to my wife and me. You can't imagine what we have been going through since our daughter ran away from home. And worse yet, we didn't know what had happened to her. We have had all kinds of thoughts, but now it is so wonderful to see her again."

It sounded almost like a broken record. I've heard that same story from so many parents. But it doesn't always have a happy ending. Some young people never go back home.

"I have been very successful in life and in business," he went on. "But, Reverend . . ." his voice cracked, and he buried his face in his hands and started to cry.

I put my hand on his shoulder, attempting to console him as best I could. Then among those tears he blurted out, "Reverend, when it comes to being a father, I'm a total failure!"

I was looking at a man at the top of the economic ladder. He was a successful businessman. He could buy almost anything he wanted. But now, because of a wayward daughter, he had been thrown off that ladder and laid at the bottom in a heap. A total failure!

"Dad," I said, patting his shoulder, "you can thank God that He has returned your daughter to you and has given you another chance. Your daughter has received Jesus as her Savior and has begun a new life in Him."

He looked at me somewhat bewildered. The message just seemed to bounce off. Then he said he was in a hurry to leave right away. Was it his resistance to the Gospel? I know it could have been his busy schedule. But it seems to me that some people are simply too busy. Anybody who doesn't have time for God certainly is too busy.

His girl got her things, and they drove away. As I stood there watching them go down our long driveway, I wondered, *Will she run away again?*

Let me tell you something, friend. I do know one thing that would have greatly helped that relationship. If I were that father and my daughter had run away, the first thing I would have done when I got home was to take her into the living room and have a little talk with her. I would immediately let my runaway daughter know what he told me—that I had failed as a father.

If something like that ever happens to you, confess your failure to your children. Now you may not own a big company or drive expensive automobiles. Maybe you can't buy just anything you want—you have to watch your pennies carefully. But I do know this: Whenever you fail, you can confess your failures to your children. Anybody can do that.

Who knows? Maybe that father did. At least the girl has never come back to the Home.

Now you know as well as I do that you have faults. It goes with the territory of being human. If you were to sit down now and make a list of your faults, it would probably be embarrassing. The list would go on and on. Do you wonder how I know that? Because I have faults too. Everybody does.

Here's something else: Our children know we have faults. But they're smart. They know if they tried to tell us about our faults, we would let them have it! We would accuse them of being sassy and disrespectful. So they know enough to keep their mouths shut about what they observe. But that doesn't change the facts. Down deep they know our faults.

What good does it do to try to hide these faults, then? Bring them out into the open. When you confess your faults, you will be amazed at how quickly your children will respond by confessing their faults to you. And it won't be long until both of you are making real turnarounds in your lives.

Someone said that the road to success is easy—just take care of your weaknesses. I think that applies to being parents. You can be a successful parent if you take care of your faults. Bring them out into the open, and let your family make a project of helping you correct them. Believe me, things will never be the same around your house after that. They will be immeasurably better!

I shall never forget something that happened when I was a small boy. I come from a poor family with eight children. My father was a garbage collector and junk man. He delivered wood, delivered fertilizer, polished cars, sold corsages. You name it, and Dad probably did it. I love him for it; he did everything imaginable to make money to support his family.

But one day—I guess I was seven or eight at the time—I came home from school and saw my father in the kitchen. It had been raining, and Dad had his feet on the oven of the wood stove. His chin hung on his chest; his eyes were closed. He looked as if he were almost dead. He said nothing when I came into the room; he didn't even stir.

Mom went to the other room, and I followed her, asking, "What's the matter with Dad?"

She put her finger to her lips and then told me, "Your father is $500 in debt."

In those days $500 seemed like $50,000 would today. Especially since we didn't have a dime in the house.

You can't imagine the fear that gripped me. I thought

this was the end of the world, that momentarily we would be thrown out on the street.

Looking back, I realize that things could have been so different if my father had simply gathered us all together and shared the problem with us. I know that would have left me with a positive impression. We all could have prayed and believed God to work things out.

But Dad never told us.

When he went on those various jobs he had to do, I was told to go along. If I had known it was for a good cause—wiping out our debts—it would have been a lot easier. Maybe I wouldn't have been so rebellious.

That's why I suggest that you sit down and make a list of your personal faults. You may want to hide them in the bottom drawer underneath everything else. It may be embarrassing if someone discovers that list. But make the list. Then begin to work on those problems. Begin to share them with your family. Then you'll be ready for the next step in bridge building.

Second, Get Your Children Involved in a Ministry With You

You will find a common bond of friendship and love when you and your children have the same motivation.

Have you ever taken your children with you when you have participated in some outreach of your church?

If more parents took their children to jail services, there would be a lot fewer children in jail today. I know a little of what jail is like. I've been there many times. But, thank God, I was always on the outside looking in.

I have been down to Skid Row in Seattle, but not on a drunken spree. I had the privilege of going down there with my father. He used to preach there because that was where he was saved. And he used to let me testify in those services.

I tried the same idea in raising my own children. I'll never forget taking Marji with me out onto the streets of New York City as we tried to reach junkies for Christ. She was probably nine or ten at the time, and this little bright spot did a lot to help us bring the Gospel to those people.

They couldn't believe a little girl would come late at night, telling them about Jesus. Marji was my drawing card.

The junkies would crowd around her and smile and offer to buy her hot chocolate. Then they would look at me. I've had them tell me that they decided I must really love them to be able to share my family with them.

Little Marji told them about Jesus. I can still see my little girl standing there in the middle of that hell telling those junkies and prostitutes that Jesus loved them. Many of them listened to her.

Our second daughter, Connie, has knelt beside many a junkie who was kicking her habit.

Once when I was coming down the hallway, I passed by what we call the kicking room, the place where the girls detoxify. I heard someone praying, and recognizing Connie's voice, I peeked in. She was on her knees, laying her hands on this terribly sick girl who was kicking her habit cold turkey.

Tears streamed down Connie's face, turned toward heaven, asking God to bring healing.

As I stood there, I couldn't help but begin to weep. It was such a beautiful sight. My little redheaded girl praying and believing God for a miracle for a sick, lonesome girl.

I joined her prayer. But I also thanked God for Connie. It was so beautiful to see her involved in our ministry too.

Our son, Jim, has always been a big brother to the girls.

He never did isolate himself but was always there, doing what he could to help meet their spiritual needs.

Now our children are grown and married. But all three still have a burden for the lost. I couldn't ask for more than that.

That's why I suggest you take your children to jail with you when you minister there. Take them with you when you visit the sick in the hospital or the aged in a rest home. Take them with you when you participate in your church's visitation program.

As you provide this common bond of service to the Lord, you will find it becomes a bond of love stronger than Elmer's glue! You will have things in common to talk about. And you will share in kingdom victories!

Third, Ask Them to Pray for You

I can almost hear you saying, "Them pray for me? Are you kidding? Won't that make me look like a weak-kneed parent? I mean, won't I be giving up parental authority?"

Not really. In fact, just the opposite will probably happen. Asking your children to pray for you becomes not a sign of weakness but of your confidence and trust in the Lord to change things. It says you believe God answers prayer.

Your children will love and respect you more than ever for this honesty. Maybe the first time it will be somewhat humbling, but you really do need their prayers.

Let me tell you about children's prayers. They are powerful! I would rather take a need to someone who is young in the faith than anyone else. I have found that to be so true at the Home. Our girls, just recently converted, have great faith in God. I have seen some miraculous answers to their prayers. Just ask our girls to pray, and things begin to happen!

The same can be true with your children. They are capable of great faith if you will let them exercise it. Start by letting them ask God to be with you and to meet your needs. A good place to begin is for them to ask God to make you the mom or dad you ought to be.

One time when our children were praying for me, they asked the Lord to help me control my temper. Wow! That was embarrassing! But I knew I was wrong. And it did give me an opportunity to apologize. After that session of praying and apologizing, a strong bond of love flowed between us.

Now here's a related method of bridge building. It may seem humiliating, but it is an exercise that can have powerful results.

Fourth, Have a "Blind Spot" Session

Blind spots are those faults we all have but may not be aware of until someone calls them to our attention.

Elsie and I have tried some sessions like this with our children. At first it got me quite upset. But I've seen it make a difference in our family.

Here's how it works: Gather the family together. This can be during your family devotional time or at some other time. Ask each member of the family to write down the others' blind spots.

When I told my family to write down my blind spots, you've never seen pencils and pens write so fast! As I sat there looking at the four of them writing, I thought, *My goodness! Don't tell me I'm that bad!*

Well, maybe I wasn't that bad, but I sure did have some blind spots that I needed to work on. Let me tell you about one of them.

I had bought a beautiful Zenith color TV. Almost everything we have is owned by the Home, and it was quite a luxury for me to have a color TV so I could watch football games. I saved my money, bought the set, and brought it home rather triumphantly.

Of course, I wasn't the only one who watched it, and the rest of the family watched things other than football. But whenever I had time to watch and a game was on, I would turn the set to that channel. Even if someone was watching something else, I would flip over to the football game without asking to see how involved they were in the program. After all, it was my set!

Well, in that blind-spot session, one of the children wrote down that they resented my turning the TV to the football game when they were in the middle of another program.

My first reaction was, "It's my TV. I can do what I want with it!" Perhaps that was true, but it certainly didn't make for harmonious family relationships!

My children had been smart enough to keep their mouths shut when I had charged in and changed channels without asking. They knew what I would tell them. So they kept quiet about it. But inside, a war had started, and resentments were building up.

Thinking back, I realized that they often got up and left when I changed channels. I had attributed that to their not being interested in football. But I was learning that the reason they walked out was the anger building up inside.

When I found out about that blind spot, I knew I was in trouble. But I also knew that the best way to solve the problem was to begin by confessing my fault to them. I also told them we would work out an arrangement whereby they could watch their programs and I could watch my football games. We each had a time slot, and that settled the matter.

Let me tell you something else. Because we were able to solve this problem together, I sensed that a stronger bond of love and understanding developed among us all.

I had other faults—other blind spots—they told me about too. But we sat down as a family and worked them out.

These blind-spot sessions have been some of the most interesting sessions we shared together. They became the basis for us to discuss each other's shortcomings in a spirit of love. We have even used family outings as a time to discuss such matters.

Try it with your family. But before you do, ask the Lord to give you wisdom and great patience. If you know how to handle it right, tremendous results will accrue to you in your family relationships.

If you're still afraid of it, let me ask you something. Isn't it a beautiful experience to have your children come and confess their faults? You gain a brighter outlook on things when your children come to you and admit they have been wrong and want to do better.

Now they're human too. And they will get a similar beautiful experience if you can share your faults with them. Your blind spots may not be apparent to you, but if you get them out in the open with your children, they will have a feeling of well-being.

Here's another closely related help in bridge building. It should be easier, but unfortunately some parents have not yet realized its value.

Fifth, Listen to Your Children

Easy? Well, to tell you the truth, it really isn't. We're all a lot better at talking than we are at listening. And many well-meaning parents never really take the time to listen to their children. The children have something to say, but the parents aren't tuned in.

I think one of the strangest cases I have ever had involved this problem.

A certain young lady, age twelve, tried to gain the attention of her father, but he just didn't have time for her. He always seemed to have more important things to do. So she felt like a third shoe.

She devised a scheme to get even with her dad for not listening. When she got through with this one, she reasoned, he'd have to listen. And he did.

Here's what happened. This young lady, I'll call her Vicki, was a fan of a writer of an advice column in the newspaper. Now, many people have been helped by this writer, and I'm not putting the column down with this illustration. I'm just telling the story to give you some idea of what happens when you don't listen to your children.

Vicki made up a story about her father's having sexual relations with her and wrote to the columnist about it, asking what she should do.

Back came the answer—the right answer. It suggested she contact the authorities to do something about the terrible problem. So Vicki went to the police with her made-up story. She told them her father was involved in incest. The police immediately arrested her father.

They lived in a small town, and the story hit the front page. It was devastating! The father was fired from his job. Even though he pleaded innocent, Vicki stuck by her story.

Then the truth came out. Vicki finally confessed it was all a big lie. But, tragically, the damage was already done.

I shall never forget her poor father. He was completely

destroyed by his daughter's lie. He just couldn't believe she would ever do something like that.

After the confession, her parents did not know what to do. They really couldn't throw a twelve-year-old out of their home, but even her presence was a constant reminder of the horrible thing she had done to them. They began to despise her. But what could you say about a little girl who was trying to get her daddy's attention?

Someone told them about the Walter Hoving Home. They called us, and Vicki received Christ as her Savior. That became the major turning point in her life.

There followed a beautiful reconciliation between Vicki and her parents. And after she was with us for a while, she was able to return home where there awaited her a complete healing in that family.

While Vicki was with us, I talked to her and learned that she had only one thing in mind in that whole lie: She wanted to get her father's attention. Well, she got his attention. But what a terrible and tragic and embarrassing— and unnecessary—way to do it!

Of course, I'm not saying that the same thing will happen to you. What I am saying is that you had better listen to your children. You can't imagine the things they will do, if they have to, to get your attention. Some, like Vicki, tell lies. Some rob. Some start using drugs. Some become immoral. And the list goes on.

So before anything like that happens, make sure you are listening to your children—and not merely to the words they say.

Now this final help in bridge building may surprise you.

Sixth, Treat Each Child as an Individual

I have heard some say that parents ought to treat all their children exactly alike—that it's wrong to play favorites. That theory may look good on paper, but it just doesn't work. And treating children differently does not mean you are favoring one over another.

Each child is different. To help each child develop his or her potential, you must devise ways to meet the needs of each child.

All three of our children are different. Every one of the hundreds of girls we have helped at the Home is different. As someone said, when God made each of us, He threw away the mold. There will never be another person exactly like you or exactly like any of your children.

What will work for and with one child may not work with and for another. You can spank one child, and that will clear the air and cure him of almost everything. But if you spank another child, you pound rebellion into a heart—and that rebellion will later explode.

One child will be corrected simply by your speaking about the situation. Another child requires more stern measures. Believe me, you can't possibly treat each child exactly the same; you must treat them as individuals, recognizing their individual differences.

One of the major causes of delinquency among our girls has been parents comparing one child with another—usually unfavorably. In a moment of frustration a parent will say, "I wish you would be good like your sister Suzie."

That's probably one of the worst things you can say. Children deeply resent that kind of comparison.

If you really are playing favorites in your home, you need to confess this fault to your family. Discuss it with your children, and ask for suggestions. You will be surprised at their answers. And be sure you deal with them as individuals.

Conclusion

If your children are growing away from you, it's up to you to build a bridge to them. You can use these helps in your bridge building:

1. Confess your faults to your children.
2. Get your children involved in a ministry with you.
3. Ask them to pray for you.
4. Have a blind-spot session to uncover problems about you that may really be irritating them.
5. Listen—really listen—to what they have to say.
6. Treat each child as an individual without playing favorites. You will need to take into consideration their differences in temperament; attitudes; emotional, physical, and social adjustments. God has made each person on earth different from every other person. He uses those differences when He deals with us, and He expects us to be aware of those differences and to take them into consideration in our dealings with one another.

Take heart. You can build that bridge. But, as I said earlier in this chapter, you have to initiate the project. And there's no better time to start than right now!

12

If a Family Prays Together, Does It Stay Together?

Volumes have been written on the value of prayer in family relationships. But there are some problems. Why is it that some families that pray together don't seem to stay together?

One of the problems of family prayer is time. Everybody is busy, busy, busy, and today's young people have activities coming out of their ears. The family is caught, pushed, pulled, torn apart by conflicting demands on its time. And while we're rushing from one activity to the next, we hear someone mouth the platitude "The family that prays together stays together." And we almost scream in response, "With all our busy schedules, how in the world do you expect us to get all the children together at one time in one place for prayer?"

I can understand that scream. I'm probably as busy as you are. And in raising our children we found that we never did *have* time to pray with them. What we had to do was to *make* time. It became a matter of priorities, and we decided that prayer had to be one of the important ones.

I believe that's what it will have to be for you too. You'll have to *make* time.

Start by analyzing all the schedules in your busy household. Make a chart if necessary. See if there are times when all members of the family could possibly be together—perhaps before or after breakfast. Or maybe it will work best for you in the evening. Try to pick a slot that has a minimum of conflicts. There is no easy way, but somehow you're going to have to do it.

Don't schedule the time in the middle of someone's favorite TV program. Or don't flip off the TV in the middle of a program—although by all means you will have to have the TV off for family devotions. Their resentment over your arbitrarily shutting off the TV in the middle of a program will overshadow any good you may accomplish!

I consider that there are two kinds of family devotions. One is where the entire family gathers together in one place at one time. This is a good starting place if you can work it out. But the ultimate goal of that kind of devotions is to bring your children to the place where they can have their own personal devotions.

Another kind of family devotions—an intermediate step—is where the parents or a parent has devotions with each child. This intermediate step can be an outgrowth of the times when the whole family is together and can be a further aid to bring the child to the place where he or she can have devotions on his own.

So if you have been feeling guilty because there is no possible way that you can get all your family members together in one place at one time, take heart. Try the intermediate step of family devotions—where you pray with each child individually, helping each to gain insights into the importance of personal devotions.

With that kind of family devotions, you also need to

keep in mind the differences in your children's personalities. Some are morning people, awakening bright and eager to face the day. Others are night people, getting up only with great reluctance and procrastination, but eager to go until the wee hours of the morning. Others are in between.

If you were to impose a strict time for devotions—where everybody had to adapt to that rigid schedule—you might well be bringing great conflict into your family. Be adaptable.

Of course, you have to teach your children the importance of regular times with God—and they must have this knowledge and instruction before they are launched out on their own. Remember your ultimate goal: to see them develop a relationship with God that will stand on its own, without any supporting crutches of your reminders or presence. They all are going to be on their own someday!

Here is another point to consider: Your children's spiritual needs will vary from child to child—and from time to time with the same child. Some seem to be able to fly immediately when they are kicked out of the spiritual nest. Others have quite a struggle being on their own.

The key is to spend all the time that you need to spend with those who are having difficulty. The others you may just need to check on once in a while.

With that in mind, I want to give you six ways you and your children can have meaningful devotional times together.

First, Discover Your Children's Weaknesses

How do you learn their weaknesses? First, just ask them. You might be surprised at what they will tell you. And as you gain their confidence, they will begin to share with you some deep-seated needs in their lives.

When they do, be careful how you handle them. For goodness sake, don't broadcast them to the rest of the family or to the church. Such confidences must be between you and your child.

After they share a weakness, pray with them about that need. Then encourage them to pray for their own need.

In the process of doing this, share with them one of your own needs. This will help them to realize that you are not a superhuman paragon of perfection—that you have problems you need to take to the Lord too. Then they will be praying for your need as well as their own during their time of devotions.

Then, every once in a while, privately check in with them to see how they are doing. This asking can even be on the fly. It is merely to show a continuing interest in their development and to remind them to keep praying until God answers.

Second, List Your Priorities

Have you ever stopped to think how many things there are that Christians can pray about? One time I went to a prayer seminar; they had hundreds upon hundreds of needs that were presented to be prayed for. That's when we face the reality that it is humanly impossible for one person to pray for every possible need. We all know there are certain things that will demand our immediate attention. These are needs that we must give priority time and attention to. So here are some suggestions for your prayer priorities.

1. Your family. Get your children in the habit of praying for each other, praying for their parents, and aware of your praying for them. Prayer does bring a bond of unity among the members of the family. If a child is upset with another member of the family, it is hard to pray for that family member. Prayer can begin the healing process because prayer changes things and people and attitudes.

Another thing: Isn't it comforting to know your name is being mentioned in prayer by someone else? I don't know if I could face all my responsibilities without that knowledge.

2. Establish goals with your children and then pray for those goals to be met.   I do hope you are teaching your children how to set goals for their lives. Why goals? Because goals bring hope.

At the Home we have a goal-setting program for our girls. They set goals for every single day that they are in school. And it is absolutely amazing to see their reactions when they have realized their goals.

You see, many of the girls who come to us have never completed anything in their lives! And that is one of the reasons they have become delinquent—their lack of accomplishment contributes to their low self-worth.

Your children may set a goal of attending summer camp. Or of getting a better grade in math. Or to gain a new friend. It could be a bicycle or an automobile. Maybe it's the salvation of a friend or to have a better disposition. The goals should not be only material ones, of course.

As you help your children establish goals, the goals can become a focus for the times of prayer you have together. God works with us as we strive toward worthy goals, and prayer helps keep those goals before us.

3. The salvation of the lost.   This is one of God's priorities. He sent His only begotten Son to provide for the salvation of the world. And the Bible tells us that He is ". ...

not willing that any should perish, but that all should come to repentance" (2 Peter 3:9).

Some of your immediate relatives may need to be converted. Put them on your prayer list. Encourage your children to pray for their cousins, aunts and uncles, grandparents, brothers and sisters. Maybe your spouse isn't saved. Children surely ought to be praying for the salvation of an unsaved father or mother.

You see, prayer has great value. When we pray about things, we tend to get involved in those things. That is why Jesus said, "Pray ye therefore the Lord of the harvest, that he will send forth labourers into his harvest" (Matthew 9:38). Jesus told us to pray because He knew that those who prayed also go into the harvest. So as you and your children begin to pray for the salvation of loved ones— even those family members who are greatly estranged from you—you will look for—and find—opportunities to share Christ with them.

4. Share with them your real needs.   Now don't make things up. And don't choose only small, insignificant matters. Whatever it is you have really been longing and praying for, share that need with your children. Let them help carry that burden.

When answers are delayed, it will help your children to see that God is not a celestial errand boy ready and eager to do whatever we tell Him to do. He is God. He is sovereign. And He knows far better than we what we need, and when we need it. Our part is to trust Him.

I don't know what it is about us parents, but we have a tendency to shield our children from our hurts. I believe this is wrong. As we share our hurts and needs, we begin to build a stronger comradeship.

And you will be surprised at how much help they will be in bearing your burdens. Don't underestimate the power of children's prayers. A woman I read about was raised from her deathbed and later came to know Christ as her Savior because her five-year-old daughter prayed simply, "Jesus, make Mommie well."

What a beautiful experience it is to have your children weep before the Lord over your needs. I tell you, that does something for you! It will make you want to be the best parent in history.

As your children weep over your needs and you weep with them over theirs, you will be drawn closely together, and your children are going to try to be the best children in the world for you.

5. Financial needs. Our financial situations vary greatly, but it seems as though almost everyone has financial needs. It is so important for our children to understand this. They need to learn to pray and trust God for finances. Their faith will be strengthened as they see God meet financial needs.

In a ministry such as ours, there are constant, recurring financial needs. There have been financial needs in our own family. As I have shared these with our children, and they prayed, we have seen God meet the need time after time. And this has helped their faith become strong as they have witnessed the miracles God has provided for our needs.

Let your children share their financial needs too and pray with them about these needs. Your faith will be boosted when God answers.

Third, Pray About Life's Partners

It's never too early to start on this. We may call it puppy love, but your teenagers may be taking a long-term look.

Your daughters will think about boys being husbands; your sons will think about girls being wives.

That's why you need to start now to pray with your teenagers about their life's partner. I know you don't want to rush the event or make it appear you are overly anxious for your children to marry, but now is the time to prepare for an event that will soon materialize in their lives.

In the course of these kinds of prayers I have found that children will ask questions. Also with continued prayer, they will seek parental approval of their friends. What beautiful opportunities to share with them the qualities of a Christian life companion.

And that points up another value of family devotions. As we share needs, we not only pray, but we also provide opportunity to have further discussions and can tell our children about the various phases of life.

Sometimes our prayer sessions have led into meaningful discussions. And that has been good for us.

Fourth, Pray for Your Pastor and Your Church

I used to be a pastor. If I became a pastor again, I have told Elsie, I would have either a large church or a small church. Here's what I mean.

In those days when I was pastoring, some of our members used to fight each other; some used to fight me. All I could do about it then was bite my tongue and cry a lot. It was hard for me to take the division among Christians.

I travel around enough to know that churches haven't changed. People are still fighting and bickering.

Well, if I were a pastor today, I would throw all those bickering people out. Then I would end up with only three or four people in church on Sundays. So if I became a pastor of a large church, it would soon become a small church. Maybe that is why God hasn't let me go back to pastoring. He knows I don't have enough patience!

But that doesn't really solve any problems, does it? Every church is made up of imperfect people. Your children need to be aware of that. After all, they are aware of the fighting and divisions. When they reach the age where they are old enough to be on their own, they may want to write the church out of their lives completely. That would be tragic. So you need to help them to see that all of us are Christians under construction. And most of us have a long way to go to become what God wants us to be!

So even though your church may have a lot of weaknesses, get them to pray for the pastor and the people. This will help them to avoid becoming bitter over the inconsistencies they see—or fancy that they see.

Instead of gossiping about pastor and people, let us make them the objects of sincere, earnest prayers in our homes.

What difference will that make? As we pray for them, God will help us to be part of the solution, not part of the problem. God will make us and our children instruments of His love to bring healing and unity back into the church.

Pastors do need a lot of prayer. Thank God for faithful pastors who are staying in there and taking so much abuse. They are true men and women of God, and we need to respect and honor them for their position in God's kingdom. Our prayers will certainly help them.

Here is another suggestion. When your children are leaving the church after the service, have them tell the pastor that they are praying for him. Stand back and watch what happens. I can almost guarantee that your pastor will be smiling from ear to ear!

Pastors sometimes have to fight great battles alone. So it

is a huge encouragement to them to know that children–
and others–are praying for them.

As your children pray about the needs of members of
the church, they will want to become involved in meeting
those needs. For example, if they pray for someone who is
sick, they may want to go and visit that person. Or they
may want to help fix some food to take to the family of the
one who is sick. If tragedy has struck a home, they may
want to go and offer some encouragement. They may even
be moved to contribute their services—such as cutting the
grass, cleaning up the yard, raking leaves, and so on.

I know this works. Some of our family's greatest opportunities to witness came when we visited the homes of people who had great needs.

I think of a family where there had been a death. We
went to pray with them, and they became our friends. A
teenage girl in another family was almost killed in an ac-
cident. We visited that family, and they have always been
extremely open toward us since then.

Prayer by itself is fine. But prayer combined with going
to meet a need will bring fantastic results.

Fifth, Prayer Can Be a Witness

Prayer at mealtime is certainly a form of family prayer.
And I hope in your family it's more than a hurried form.

Do you also use prayer as a witness when you're out in
public?

At the Home, because we eat cafeteria style, each person
bows his or her head and prays a silent prayer.

I consider our children well-balanced. But I want to
tell you something they do in public. Not only do they
bow their heads and close their eyes, but our married children have asked us to join hands with them around the

table in a restaurant, and then have asked someone to pray out loud.

They aren't ashamed of their Christian witness. Even though once in a while I may get a little embarrassed, down deep inside I am proud of the way they acknowledge God when they thank Him for their food, no matter where they are.

After a situation like this, I have had people come up to us and commend us for praying in public. One couple, tears sparkling in their eyes, told me it was one of the most beautiful sights they had ever witnessed. I didn't have a chance to talk to them, but I suspected their children had cut them off. And that is so sad.

Prayer around the dinner table—at home or out in public—can be a blessed experience. And is it not another witness to our faith in Christ?

Sixth, Memorize Scripture

Praying is much more than asking God for things. Family devotions should include more than prayer. It should also include a time with God's Word.

One way to make God's Word come alive for your children is to memorize it together. They may be able to do that better than you, but no matter. It is important at every age to hide God's Word away in our hearts.

But rote learning is not enough. They also need to live out the Scripture they memorize. Memorization and personalization will help them build their faith in God.

A number of years ago the Teen Challenge ministry was suffering growing pains. (Our Home is a Teen Challenge girls' home, and we too were in that pattern of growth.)

But with the growth, some weaknesses became evident. Some directors, with a sincere desire to encourage growth, tried to analyze exactly what was the best way to cure drug addicts, alcoholics, and delinquents.

Strange things happened. Some directors began to use the methods of the world. Some group-encounter sessions became times when young people lost their tempers. They called this getting it all out.

Other well-meaning counselors began to dwell on the past in minute detail. These sessions became terribly embarrassing to those who came to us for help.

I honestly didn't know what to do. I certainly wanted to have the best possible methods of helping these young people, yet I felt uneasy about the emphasis on psychological methods.

David Wilkerson, founder of Teen Challenge, with whom I traveled for a number of years as crusade director, was conducting a meeting in Ohio. I was so confused about the whole situation that I decided to go out and talk to him about methods.

One afternoon when we sat down together, I asked him the question that had been bothering me for months: "How do we really help the young people who are addicts, alcoholics, and delinquents?"

Without a moment's hesitation, David Wilkerson replied, "John, it's the promises of God."

He went on to explain that rehabilitation of these people should not be complicated, but should be founded on God's Word through His promises.

I came back determined to share with the girls the power of God's Word. At that time we started something that we continue to this day at the Home—Scripture memorization—and plenty of it.

In fact, the first thing in the morning, right after breakfast, we each take a promise for the day from the promise box. Then three girls will read aloud their promises while we are all assembled.

Feeling a deep spiritual need in my life, I began to memorize the Scriptures, personalizing and trying to live them. I memorized hundreds of verses, using them as a basis for Christian living. When I did that, things came together in this ministry. We continued to grow, and God began to meet our needs.

To this day I have kept that activity up. And I plan to do it until Jesus comes.

So encourage your children to memorize portions of Scripture. Memorization, of course, should not be an end in itself. After we memorize, then we practice what we have memorized. I call that living the Scripture.

Let me tell you something else about the promises of God. Sometimes when I am memorizing a verse, I suddenly gain an overwhelming insight into it. It's really an emotional experience for me.

I have learned two things about Scripture. If God gives me a verse and it really comes to mean something to me, then I know that on up ahead I will need that verse for some spiritual battle. It's as if God is giving me the ammunition I'll need to shoot down the enemy in some future battle.

Or something else happens. I have found that in the middle of a battle while I am groping for some kind of help or assurance, the Lord will give me a passage of Scripture. I will memorize it, and it will take me through to victory.

I have learned that God's Word either helps to prepare us for battle, or it will carry us through in the midst of battle.

Unfortunately some well-meaning Christians have no armament for battle. Since they don't know the promises of God, they struggle and struggle and struggle. I hope you aren't like that. And I hope you have begun to help your children put their faith and trust in God's Word.

Be sure to memorize the verses your children are working on. That way you can relate to them how you put into practice in your life what the verse is teaching. Then let them tell you how they are doing. You will be amazed at what they will learn from this.

Conclusion

I had a beautiful experience not too long ago, when I was visiting the home of one of our married children. As I was sitting in the living room, I noticed them having prayer with their child. How I thanked God for that. What Elsie and I tried to instill in them is now being passed on to their children.

I am praying that will happen to you too. The strongest spiritual fortress in America is the family. If you have taught your children to have devotions, when they get out on their own, they will stay true to the Lord. And how happy you will be to see the results that have come from your taking time with them.

If you don't take time with your children now, then you will be forced to take time with them later. And let me tell you from my experience of working among delinquent girls, it's much better to make the time to pray with them when they are smaller.

Prayer is one of your major weapons in raising your children. And prayer will be one of the great secrets of victory in their lives. So you need to teach them to pray.

Remember those six ways to keep prayer in focus in your family:

1. Discover your children's weaknesses.

2. List your priorities for your family.
3. Pray about life's partners.
4. Pray for your pastor and the members of your church.
5. Pray over your meals—at home and in public—as a reminder of God's provisions for you.
6. Top all this off by memorizing and personalizing God's promises so that they can be a vital part of your prayer and life.

Prayer *can* indeed keep your family together.

13

Should I Make My Children Go to Church?

Church attendance is another difficult question. Believe me, there are no simple answers.

Some young people who have been forced to go to church declare, "When I get older, I won't go to church."

I know they say that; I was one of them.

Church was a part of my family's life when I was growing up. In fact, every Sunday we went to church five times! To do that, we left early in the morning and drove twenty-two miles and at night drove the twenty-two miles home. Sunday was church day—all day. And I hated it.

When I grow up, I told myself, *I am going to be a Presbyterian.* There were two reasons for that decision. The first was that my girl friend at that time was Presbyterian. The second was that I had visited her church, and the services were short. I liked that.

Now things didn't work out that way. I later broke off with that girl friend, and I met the most beautiful girl in all the world; she is now my wife.

And I didn't end up a Presbyterian—although I have nothing against them and their church. They are wonderful people. But God led me to become an Assemblies of God minister.

Would you believe that today I go to church every Sunday—and like it? Maybe not five times—but for me Sunday is a beautiful day with the Lord.

Does that mean my parents were right in making me go to church? And how does that relate to the question of this chapter: "Should I make my children go to church?"

Suppose your child is 6 feet 9 inches and weighs 250 pounds, a star football player. Are you asking me if you should march into that boy's bedroom on Sunday morning, throw that hulk out of bed, and tell him he has to go to church?

If you're faced with that kind of problem, you have two choices: Wake him up and run for your life, or stand your ground and be ready to be eaten alive!

So before answering the question, let's try to understand the problem. Some church services are a bore to young people. The singing is foreign to their life-style and experience. The preaching is dull and not related to their questions. The preacher uses illustrations about steamships instead of spaceships. And the whole service is primarily ritual.

The tragic thing about that kind of situation is that your children may know you go to church because of ritual—because it's the accepted thing to do. And they see right through that.

On the other hand, we know that children need to attend church. Hebrews 10:25 warns us about "not forsaking the assembling of ourselves together. . . ." Our life in Christ depends on sustenance we receive in the church. It's a part of our spiritual strength and growth. So here are four ways that will help you answer the question about making your children go to church.

First, Ask Your Children Why They Don't Want to Go to Church

They'll probably give you the classic answers. I've heard them often. In fact, I know them quite well because these are some of the excuses I used to give my parents.

I would say, "There are a bunch of phonies in that church." Or, "I don't get anything out of it." Or, "If you make me go to church, I'll run away from home." (I never did.)

I used to recite all the shortcomings of the people at the church. One time I really had my parents over a barrel. I caught the pastor using a dirty, four-letter word! Poor fellow, he was totally exasperated with us ornery kids, and he shouted out a word that had no place in a Christian's vocabulary. Did I ever laugh on the inside at him!

I told my mom about it and said I thought I should keep my distance from someone who talked like that. But it didn't work. I still had to go to church.

Even though you'll get those timeworn answers, go ahead and ask your children why they don't want to go to church. You will give them a chance to vent their feelings. They have such feelings, and they must get them out into the open.

As they run down their long list of why they shouldn't go, just stand there and bite your tongue. What they are saying is probably what they are believing. And since the church is partly a human institution, it does have its weaknesses. There are phonies. There are pastors who use four-letter words when they are exasperated. And at times church is a bore. I remember that when I was growing up, the music sometimes seemed so ancient that I didn't think even the angels would sing some of the hymns.

But as they answer your question, don't interrupt. Listen.

After they get through, ask them if they have anything else to say about their not going. They probably will. In fact, they'll probably be terribly excited that at last you've decided to listen to reason! So let them get it all out.

I am not a psychiatrist, but I am told that people who vent their feelings become very vulnerable. In other words, after they get all their anger out, then you can get your point across; they're ready to listen. But you can't do it until they get it all out.

Second, Ask Them for Suggestions to Improve the Church's Ministry

Don't attempt to respond, point by point, to their reasons for not wanting to go to church. Instead just ask something like, "If you were the pastor, what would you do to improve the church?"

Depending on the nature and age of your children, you may get another long list. Agree with what they are saying—if it is the truth. And make comments like, "That's a good suggestion."

This is a principle from the business world. They call it participative management.

I once had the wonderful opportunity to attend a week-long seminar of the American Management Association. One of our advisory boards is a member group of that association, and they were able to give me a scholarship to attend the seminar.

For a whole week I sat down with the presidents of companies from around the country. I was the only preacher, of course. Some of these men flew in, in their own private jets, and I was really a fish out of water. But I sat and listened. And I learned.

We studied the principle of participative management. Essentially it involves letting those people who are involved in the actions make decisions relative to those actions.

Having learned this principle, I wanted to see if it really worked. So back at the Home I picked the kitchen.

I guess the kitchen must be one of the hardest parts of any ministry. People complain about institutional food, and the cooks have a difficult time taking that criticism. I suppose I have spent more time encouraging the cooks than almost anybody else. And I have always felt sorry for them. So to see if this principle would work, I decided to start in the hardest place—the kitchen.

I asked Elsie, who is director of our food services, to gather together all the girls involved in the cooking. Then I had each of these girls work out a menu. Of course, Elsie made sure they were balanced meals.

After they had figured out what should be on the menus, they went into the kitchen and prepared the food they had decided to cook. But there was a difference now. Before, the head cook had decided the menus, and the other girls simply helped her. Now everybody who was cooking also was involved in making the decisions about what should be served.

The principle worked beautifully. Those girls knocked themselves out cooking because they had had some input into what should be cooked.

That is essentially what participative management is: letting the people who do the work become involved in making the decisions on their level.

Now back to the church. If people had the opportunity to apply this principle in the church, I believe it would work wonders. And the suggestions your children make might be the beginning of getting them involved in the activities of the church.

This leads naturally into my third suggestion.

Third, Ask the Pastor to Give Your Children Church Responsibilities

It is amazing how we change our attitudes toward organizations or ministries when we are actively involved in them. Your children will criticize the church loudly if they are on the fringes looking in. But if they are on the inside looking out, it will be different.

Your pastor is probably waiting for you to come with such a request. People today are so busy that most churches have far more tasks to be done than there are willing workers to do them.

Getting your child involved in the activities of the church will do three things: (1) It will help build the kingdom of God; (2) It will bring recognition to your child; (3) It will provide great learning experiences.

One of the great mysteries of most churches is the church board meeting. What in the world goes on in board meetings? Some of them seem to last forever. What do they talk about?

You can usually pick out the board members of the church: They stand around with stern faces. They almost seem like members of the CIA. Is it the secretive nature of the meetings that changes the expressions of otherwise normal human beings?

If I ever went back to pastoring, I would open some sessions of the church board to the public. I would especially want young people there to observe.

Now if you are a board member and you're reading this, you're probably protesting that you couldn't let the young people in because there's too much fighting.

Well, maybe if you let them in, you wouldn't fight so much! Rather than losing tempers over what color to paint the sanctuary, you'd learn to control yourself for the sake of the young people. I think that would help.

Some forward-looking companies in the business world are allowing more outsiders into the internal functions of their organizations. And they are quite successful as a result. Why aren't we doing this in the church?

Now, of course, I know there are some things which the board must discuss in private. You could take care of those in another meeting.

"Sunshine laws" have opened up agencies of the government so that the public can attend their meetings and know what is going on. Should the church be the last to follow? I believe that as we open our churches more to input from all the people, our churches will become stronger.

Maybe our children could be appointed to various committees in the church—and not just in figurehead appointments either. I mean in a way that is functional, where they are really involved in doing the job.

Involvement is the key. Get people involved, and you have their loyalties. But let them stand on the fringes, and they will continue to criticize. I guess it is the truth of that old Indian proverb: I will not criticize another until I have walked a day in his moccasins.

So get your children involved in the inner workings of the church, and they will soon begin to change their minds about the church. If they can see their pastor in the heat of a board meeting, they will start praying for him, rather than criticizing him.

If they could understand that the church parking lot cannot be lighted simply because there are no funds available for this project, they will stop complaining about the darkness—and may even start to organize some fundraising projects to buy and install the lights.

And that brings me to my fourth suggestion. If you're not sitting down, I suggest you do so before you read this. It may shock you.

Fourth, If Necessary, Change Churches

If you are a pastor reading this, please stay with me. Because what I am suggesting here is the last resort. And I do mean *last.*

Some churches in America are so bad that young people will never have a chance in them. Their services are dull and boring and have no spiritual life whatsoever. That's not God's fault; it's the fault of the people. Unfortunately, the chances of your changing a situation like that are almost nil. So, change churches.

Some churches have ongoing, lively programs. People who have gone from lifeless churches into churches like that have told me that the change in their children has been remarkable. They get on fire spiritually. Those parents say that changing churches was one of the best decisions they ever made.

But, this has got to be your last resort. Make sure you run through all the previous suggestions before you try this one.

If you decide you must change, I assume you will look for a church that believes in the salvation of the lost and in the infilling of the Holy Spirit. One of the other questions you will want to ask is what kind of youth program they have. I am proud to say that I know of many forward-looking churches that have great youth programs. That may be the answer to your problem.

With this background, I think we are ready to tackle that question: *Should I make my children go to church?*

The church can do more for our youth than can schools, museums, hamburgers, or football. So why shouldn't we make the decision about whether or not they will attend church?

We make other decisions for our children. We tell them they have to eat their spinach, go to bed, be in bed at a certain time, do their homework. We don't believe they are mature enough to simply do what they want to do. But yet when it comes to the most important matter of all, some people think that their children ought to make the decision for themselves as to whether or not they will go to church.

Why is church so important? The more we expose our youth to Christ-centered activities, the greater are the chances of their living for Jesus. If they aren't in church, how can they be challenged to live for Christ?

I was showing one of my films at a church a while back. God's spirit was evident in our midst, and we had a tremendous altar service. God really touched lives that night.

After the service as I was walking down the church aisle to go to my car, a woman stopped me. "Oh, please help me," she begged. "I can't handle my teenage daughter anymore."

This poor woman was really distraught, crying.

I turned to look for the daughter. No one was in sight. "Where is your daughter?" I asked.

"She's at home."

When I asked her why the daughter wasn't in church, the mother replied, "She doesn't want to come to church."

And that was the problem.

I know I may not be the greatest filmmaker in the world, but I do make films that are exciting to young people. I believe I would have had a much better chance of reaching that daughter for Christ if she had been in the service that night.

Possibly the mother didn't believe in making her daughter go to church. Maybe the daughter said she didn't want to go—that church was dumb—and the mother accepted that answer. But that is not the answer we are looking for.

Some well-meaning parents say they let their teenage children make all their own decisions. That reminds me of a time when I was talking to a man about his son. What I knew, that he didn't know, was that his son was on drugs. And the boy had become a pusher. I shall never forget what the father told me. He proudly boasted that he let his son make all his own decisions.

That's dangerous. Teenagers aren't ready to make decisions for which they don't have enough intelligence or experience to make the *right* decisions.

You have to make some decisions for them. So as far as you are concerned, one of the things that your children must do is go to church.

If you haven't made it one yet, let that be a rule in your family: *On Sunday we go to church.* Of course, if you personally only go to church occasionally and make excuses to stay home frequently, you have a real problem. You can't expect your children to go. And, please, don't send the children and stay home yourself. That is one of the worst examples. You take them.

If your children are small, somewhere along the line they will tell you they don't want to go to church. But just tell them right out front that in your house everybody goes to church. Let that be a habit just as eating dinner is a habit. It is just one of the things that everybody in the household does. Under no circumstances does anyone violate that habit.

As the children get older, it may have to be a little stronger. Tell them that as long as they are going to live in your house, they will always go to church. And that's it. Let them know, and clearly, that the whole family goes to church on Sundays.

Conclusion

If you are having problems with your children not wanting to attend church, follow these steps:

1. Ask your children why they don't want to go to church Don't respond to their excuses or accusations; just let them vent their feelings.
2. Ask for their suggestions on how they would improve the church situation.
3. Ask your pastor to give them specific responsibilities in the church.
4. As a last resort, if your church is dead and dull and has no appeal to young people, you may have to consider changing to a church that is alive, vital, and interested in youth. But that kind of decision must be made only after a great deal of prayer.

Make it clear to your children that church attendance is a regular family activity and they are expected to attend.

Mom and Dad, I encourage you to join the back-to-church crusade. I know it pleases the heart of God to see all the members of the family in church—together.

14
Coping With Rebellious Teens

Have you ever felt like screaming at your child to shut up? Or, worse still, slapping him in the face for sassing you? We both know that isn't the way to cope with rebellious teens, but I sure do know how you feel!

Let me share with you some of my thoughts on how to handle rebellious teenagers.

First, Decide What Kind of Punishment to Give

I believe children need to be spanked. Proverbs 22:15 says: "Foolishness is bound in the heart of a child; but the rod of correction shall drive it far from him."

But my belief in spanking is conditional: Be sure they are children. Little children should be spanked. But if you try spanking older teens, you may end up picking yourself up off the floor!

Here's something else you really have to be careful of: Be sure you know the difference between spanking and beating.

There was actually a case in New York in which a child

went to the authorities after a spanking. The authorities saw black and blue marks and arrested the parents.

Now I'm not saying it's illegal to spank your children, but there's a hue and cry today—most of it justified— about child beating. It really makes me cringe to see how some children have been abused. I am completely on the side of the law in these cases.

But just as with anything else, there can always be extremes. God forbid if it ever does become illegal to spank our children, as it has become in some countries.

You probably know the difference between spanking and beating, but let me give you my definition. Spanking is the intelligent exercise of punishment for something that's gone wrong. Beating is venting your own anger in an uncontrolled manner. And that makes a child rebellious.

After you spank a child, be sure to throw your arms around him or her and love that erring one. Spanking to some children carries the overtones of alienation of affection. You don't want that. So after you spank them, be sure to let them know you still love them and care for them deeply. If you hug them, they are reassured of your love.

Sometimes I am asked at what age parents should stop spanking and start to rely solely on reasoning. That's a difficult one since children are so different. But it seems to me that when they are around twelve years of age, it's time to stop spanking. If you are in doubt about your child, the Lord will certainly guide you in this important decision.

We have a saying at the Home: "Fit the punishment to the crime." Not all crimes require the same punishment. You may get really upset because of some things your children have done wrong, but don't let your anger determine the punishment.

Some thoughtful parents have even asked the children what kind of punishment they need. Children are usually harder on themselves than you are on them. I tried this idea with our children, and it really works. It has worked with the girls at the Home too.

For teenagers, try a denial of privileges. With my Jim it was sports. Not letting him go out and play with the kids was catastrophic as far as he was concerned. That punishment worked wonders—and prevented some offenses.

The punishment could be extra hours of working around the house. The trick is to try to find the most effective means of punishment for each child and to stick with it.

Don't ever forbid your children to attend a church activity as a punishment. I hope by this time it's obvious to you that when they go to church activities, they are being exposed to the convicting power of the Holy Spirit—and that will do more than any punishment you could possibly devise. Church is where you want them.

If my child had been disobedient, instead of forbidding attendance at the church activity, I would call the youth pastor or youth leader to let him know I was sending my child and that I had been having problems. As my child went to that activity, I would pray that the Lord would use the leader to help reach my child. Sometimes young people are able to relate better to someone other than their parents. God can use such a person to take out rebellion.

Also, don't ever deny them food as punishment. You can get yourself into problems with the authorities on that!

When you have more than one child in the home, you can't always give the same kind of punishments. One child may need a certain type of punishment for the offense, while another child may need an entirely different kind of punishment for the same offense.

When a child begins to yell that his brother or sister only got so-and-so, when he got such-and-such, then you need to explain that you felt you gave each the kind of punishment that was needed. Let this be an opportunity to discuss differences in personality and degrees of punishment. Reassure them you will always try to give them just the right amount of punishment, that you're not playing favorites. And be sure you're not!

Second, Make the Rules Clear-cut

Your children are supposed to be in by 10:00 P.M. and they arrive at 10:30. Now they will give you a million excuses for being late. Once in a great while they may even give you a reason. What should you do?

Elsie and I have had rules about what time our children should be in. We required them to call us if they were going to be later than the agreed-upon time. If there was no call, then they were punished for being out late.

Other rules in the household should be just as clear. I don't see this as setting up a prison. In fact, you can sit down with your children and let them help make the rules. At least get them to agree to them. Then when the rules are violated, it is much easier for them to understand their punishment.

I hope I am not overusing the word *punish*. At the Home we don't call it punishment; we call it loving discipline. It is a combination of love and discipline.

When you explain the rules to your teens, don't say, "That's the rule, and I expect you to obey it. And I don't want any argument over it."

There are two things wrong with that approach: (1) The child doesn't understand the reason behind the rule, and (2) the arrogance of the parent brings out rebellion in the child.

All our rules need to have legitimate explanations. I

know that some disagree with me on this. They say that rules are rules, and children are to obey them without question.

That reasoning may appeal to some authoritarians, but I have learned that I spend less time defending a rule that has been properly defined or accepted than in trying to make a rule and enforce it when there has been no explanation.

So explain the reasons behind your rules. That's something like a curve sign on a highway. If drivers disregard curve signs, they plunge off the road and may be killed. Curve signs are safety rules to keep us alive and well. It's the same with rules in the home. And good rules have good reasons behind them.

Be positive about the rules; try to eliminate negative aspects. For example, don't say that your children can't be out after 10:00 P.M. Say it positively: "You will be in by ten." Don't say, "You can't sleep in on Sunday morning." Say, "You will go to church on Sunday morning." Don't say, "If you don't mow the grass, you can't go to the football game." Say, "If you mow the grass, you can go to the game." Keep it positive.

Third, Don't Get Caught in the Trap of Using Force Against Force

If your child yells at you, don't yell back. If he strikes at you, don't strike back. Romans 12:17 says to repay no one evil for evil. And that applies to parents too.

We also read: "Be not overcome of evil, but overcome evil with good" (Romans 12:21). The Revised Standard Version translates that, "Remain calm." That can be tough!

Parents have to learn to speak rationally, not in anger

or with violence. Some parents, even so-called Christian parents, have resorted to violence. It never works.

Do you know where more beatings take place than any other place in America? In the ghettos. Kids are beaten unmercifully by parents who were beaten when they were children. And those kids grow up to rob and kill and destroy—and to beat their children. It's such a senseless waste. Beatings have never accomplished what reasonable correction can do.

So if you feel a burst of anger, turn around and walk away. Collect your thoughts and emotions; then come back and sit down and talk with your children rationally and logically. If punishment is warranted, let it be what I have referred to as loving discipline.

Fourth, Consider if You're Responsible for Their Rebellion

Here's another good Scripture verse for you: "Fathers, provoke not your children to wrath" (Ephesians 6:4).

I know of cases where teenagers are rebellious because of their parents.

You have probably seen sassy little brats. I have. Do you know where they got that sassiness? From their parents. If you're around their parents long enough, you'll hear them sassing their children. And it doesn't take long for little imitators to pick that up.

If you yell at your children, it won't be long before they will start yelling back at you.

Are you constantly on their backs? Nitpicking? Nagging? Yelling? Overbearing? Demanding? Let me tell you, if you keep those things up, you are going to have rebellious children.

Follow that scriptural advice: "Provoke not your children to wrath."

Here's a little family activity you might want to try. Have a session with your children and call it, "What's Bugging You?"

Before you go into such a session, you may want to spend some time in prayer because you may be in for a few jolts. But if in this session you create the right environment for your children to express their true feelings, you may be absolutely amazed at what is bugging them.

They may tell you they can't stand your yelling. Or they can't stand your nagging and nit-picking and demanding. They can't stand the way their parents shout at each other.

Are you still with me? As I told you, you had better be prayed up before this session because it will be a real eye-opener. But I believe you will see some tremendous results from it. If you are the cause of the rebellion, it will help mend that situation so you can be reconciled with your child.

Give your children an opportunity to express themselves. And keep your heart open, your ears open, your eyes open—and your mouth shut!

Fifth, Do Something Now to Prevent Rebellion in the Future

Younger children will take discipline without responding. But after years of pent-up emotions, they are likely to explode.

I don't consider myself a child psychologist, but some of these observations come from common sense. I have seen it so much in the girls at the Home.

By the time the girls who have come to us became older teenagers, they couldn't take anymore in their own homes. So they ran away. Some of them became drug addicts and prostitutes. Why? It was all those pent-up emotions that grew through years of parental abuse.

Good discipline requires large doses of love and understanding. Can you honestly say you feel the hurt the way your children feel the hurt? Your discipline was supposed to train them in righteousness. Did it?

When was the last time you cried with your children? I tell you, you are a real parent if you learn to cry with them. If you have to punish them, do it, and then weep when they are weeping. Tell them you are terribly disappointed and that it hurts deep down inside. Tears have a way of washing out anger and rebellion. They certainly have for me.

I am not ashamed that I have cried with my children. At times it was embarrassing. Sometimes I felt uncomfortable. But I have asked God to help me feel their pain and suffering. Crying is not the sign of a sissy. Crying is feeling pain.

Teach your children that rebellion against their parents is actually rebellion against God. Just a word of caution, though. Don't use God as a threat. This may cause your children to form a wrong, but lasting, impression of God as hard and angry. Teach them the results of rebellion, but in relationship to the total character of God.

Your life and attitude will affect those of your children. That's why the Bible says: "The just man walketh in his integrity [moral soundness, honesty, uprightness]: his children are blessed after him" (Proverbs 20:7).

Sixth, Help Them to Discover God's Plan for Their Lives

God has a beautiful plan for every life. How do your children discover that plan? Do you know for yourself? One of the great adventures for every Christian is to discover God's plan for his life. Life will take on new meaning when he does, and he will look forward to the activities of the day with new appreciation and anticipation.

Here are five thoughts you can share with your children on how to discover God's plan for their lives.

1. Believe God has a plan for your life. That may sound simple, but it is the basis of your discovery. You must be convinced God does have a plan before you can find it.

Let me illustrate it this way. A study of the universe shows us that God has a plan for the sun, moon, and stars. We see God's plan in earth's vegetation and animal kingdom. If God has a plan for all the other parts of His creation, surely He has a plan for us.

The events in the Garden of Eden reveal God's plan for Adam and Eve: to multiply and replenish the earth. That was part of God's plan for their lives.

Remember the excitement of God's plan for the children of Israel? Freedom from Egypt and a miraculous journey to Canaan.

The Gospels disclose in detail Christ's plan for His twelve disciples. Then Christ revealed His master plan for all of us in Mark 16—winning the lost.

I hope that you are beginning to believe that God is interested in you, that He does have a plan for your life.

My father's natural calling was to witness to individuals and win them to Christ. He talked to gas-station attendants, waitresses, hitchhikers, neighbors, and almost everyone with whom he came in contact.

My secret desire was to be a great soul winner like my father. I tried to do what he had done—witnessing to this person and that person, but somehow I just didn't "have it." The harder I tried, the more discouraged I became.

One Sunday morning I was sitting in church with my

wife and the girls from our Home. The pastor was preaching on the importance of soul winning. As he preached, I felt guilty. I wasn't doing my part. I felt that compulsion to go out and knock on doors.

I knew, however, that the moment I got out there, I would face the same failure I had faced so many times before.

As I sat there listening to our pastor, the Holy Spirit began to speak to my heart. The Lord knew that in my frustration and discouragement I needed something. So He told me to look ahead of me. I saw our girls sitting in the rows just ahead of us. In a gentle, reassuring way God said that His plan for me was to be the director of a home for those girls.

Possibly you have felt the same way I did—guilty because you weren't doing what some other Christian was doing. But God's plan for you may not be for you to be a great soul winner.

Maybe as a young person growing up you went forward in church to dedicate your life to missionary service. But as time and circumstances passed by, that didn't work out. Now as you are reading this, you may still have a sense of guilt—as though you have missed God's will. My friend, all is not lost! God still has a good plan for your life. It may not be the mission field. It may not include going door-to-door and witnessing. It may be some other worthwhile and beneficial service that you can do well for the glory of God.

2. God's plan is a part of your daily activities. One discovery I made about God's plan is that it involves today. God gives us a special tool—love—to be used not at some point in the distant future, but today.

Is a neighbor of yours having a lot of problems? Do you go over and show love by helping with a project? When you drive out your driveway and your neighbor is struggling with a flat tire, do you stop and offer to help? If someone in the neighborhood has died, do you send a note of concern to let the family know you are praying for them? And do you show your concern in a practical way by taking over a casserole?

There are many practical, down-to-earth ways you can show God's love to others. That's part of God's plan for you.

Love seems to be going out of style in our world and is being replaced by hate. This means there is a greater opportunity than ever for us Christians to become involved by using God's special tool—love. Jesus said that love would be the badge whereby others would know that we are His disciples.

3. God's plan involves people. Christ is people centered. As we become a tool of love in God's hands, we too become people centered.

At our Home we have dinners and invite the unsaved. Sometimes we invite celebrities who, in many circumstances, are otherwise unreachable. They may never go to church, but they will come to a dinner at our Home.

When we get them there, we have more than a meal. Some of our girls testify and share with them what Jesus has done in their lives. It is surprising the impression this makes on our visitors.

Was the last time you were involved in church or other activities something that touched the hearts of the unsaved?

4. Good will always come our way in God's plan. The Lord rewards His workers. When Adam and Eve were in the Garden of Eden, everything was provided for them. They didn't have to worry about the necessities of life. God took care of that.

When the Israelites fulfilled God's plan by journeying to

Canaan, God gave them food and water in the barren wilderness. Even their shoes and clothes didn't wear out all those years!

I remember when I first went to work for David Wilkerson. He told me, "John, there are a lot of things you will have to give up—a lot of things. But God will always more than make it up to you."

That was many years ago, and I have seen his statement fulfilled many times over. God has indeed been good to us. He has supplied everything we need.

Yes, you can expect that good will come your way as God works out His plan in your life. After all, He is your loving Heavenly Father.

5. God's plan keeps us close to Jesus.   When we have discovered God's plan for our lives and when we use that tool of love, we will encounter difficulties. Many times we are driven to our knees. Sometimes we will be misunderstood and feel like giving up. During those moments we will become aware of the nearness of Jesus Christ. There is nothing so reassuring as to know that Jesus stands with us.

This plan I have been talking about is not our plan. It is God's plan. And as we discover His plan, we will find that because it is His plan and He works through His Son, His plan will draw us ever so close to Jesus.

Remember what Jesus said: "He who is faithful in little is faithful also in much." So begin today to follow God's plan. Use His love. You will be amazed at the avenues that it opens for you.

Conclusion

You can overcome rebellion by being ready to face it. Remember that these suggestions can help you:

1. Decide what kind of punishment to give, remembering that it will have to vary according to the person and the situation.
2. Make the rules clear-cut and stick with them.
3. Don't use force against force.
4. See if you are the reason for the rebellion and take steps to be reconciled with your child.
5. Do something to prevent rebellion, and learn to weep in sympathy with your children.
6. Help your children discover God's will for their lives, and set the example for them by demonstrating God's love in your world.

Looking back on those suggestions, you may realize that you have a lot of work to do. But God will be faithful to you. He wants to help you take that rebellion out of your children.

15

How to Enjoy Your Children

Do you still have fun with your children? Or are you eagerly anticipating the day when they will be grown and gone?

Some parents long to be free. But many others want to keep their children around as long as possible. Those parents have discovered that children are indeed a blessing to be enjoyed, not a bane to be tolerated.

Here are some ways to help you enjoy your children.

First, Seek Their Advice

I can almost hear your, "Are you kidding? My kids don't have an ounce of sense!"

Now wait a minute. Don't you know that children today are more educated and generally more mature than we were at their age? If you think I'm wrong, just try helping them with their homework!

I also think this generation of young people is more spiritual than previous generations. Maybe that isn't true among those you know. Maybe you were a very spiritual person when you were growing up and you notice a lack of spirituality among your children.

But in my observations, working among thousands of young people, I find them today to have a real touch of God upon their lives. And they are eager to share the Gospel with others. They are concerned about world conditions; they really want to use their lives for Christ and His work.

In my denomination Bible schools are bulging with young people wanting to learn to be effective workers in the harvest.

So I believe our children have some things they can tell us. The problem is that we are not listening when they are talking. Our attitude seems to be: After all, they're only children; what can they tell us?

Next time you're facing a problem, why not go to them, spell it out, and ask them what they would do about it. The Bible talks about situations like that. It says that in the multitude of counselors there is safety (Proverbs 11:14).

I have tried this with my own children and with the girls who come to our Home, and I am absolutely amazed at their answers. They are right on target. It overwhelmed me because I really didn't expect it to be that way. I discovered that young people are thinking and are rational. They do have advice they can share with us to help us.

Another thing. Your going to them for advice tells them you think they are worth something. Remember how you felt that last time someone came to you and asked for your advice? You gave them that advice and had a nice, warm feeling toward them as a result.

Children are people too. Granted, they may not yet be prophets, professors, or perfect. Some of their advice will miss the mark by a mile. But still they will feel good about you and about themselves if you give them the opportunity to help you with your problems.

Have you ever been in any brainstorming sessions? Brainstorming is a tool used by businesses and other organizations to get a lot of ideas on how to solve a problem. There is one basic rule for brainstorming to be effective: Whatever ideas are given, no one can criticize them. Even if they are off the wall and ridiculous, they are not evaluated or criticized. The point is to record as many ideas as possible. Evaluation comes later. At this point nothing is permitted to stymie the free flow of ideas.

I think that would be a good rule for a family. When you get together and someone offers an idea, don't immediately squelch it. Just nod your head and smile and keep the way open for more ideas. A seemingly ridiculous idea may generate a workable idea. Also I have found that the person who offers an unworkable idea soon realizes that it isn't very good.

When you're asking your children for advice, you're trying to encourage a free flow of ideas. Don't put their suggestions down immediately. Give them time.

There's something else this procedure will do. As your children come up against life's problems, they will seek answers to them rather than running from them—because you have set a pattern for them.

I'm sure you're acquainted with Jesus' promise: "All things are possible to him that believeth" (Mark 9:23). But do you really believe that? If you do, you need to instill it in your children. Teach them that every problem has a solution and that nothing is accomplished by running from problems.

Believe it, act upon it, and share problems with your children so they can see how God works to help you come up with solutions.

When you hit a dead end in your strength, it is a great opportunity for God to answer and show you the way.

I remember when Jim wanted a special pair of shoes—when those with the slightly higher heels for men first came out. I didn't have the money to buy them. But we believed together that "all things are possible."

Now this wasn't all that easy to be answered. First, Jim was praying for a particular style of shoes. Second, Jim has a very wide foot, and fitting him was difficult.

Later someone came by the Home with clothing for the girls. They told me they knew it was a girls' home but wondered if anybody could use a pair of men's shoes.

I looked at the shoes in amazement. They were stylish—with the higher heel; they were wide.

You probably have guessed it. Those shoes fit Jim perfectly.

I tell you, my faith was boosted. And you should have seen Jim when he put them on. His eyes were big as saucers! And he had learned a great lesson—a lesson far more important than the shoes themselves. He had learned that God answers prayer.

Since we know nothing is impossible with God, let's take on some big projects. Share the problem with your children, and some of them will say, "Well, Dad and Mom, why don't we pray about it? I believe God can answer."

You will sit back in amazement. The works of faith are beginning to be evident in your children.

Second, Make a List of Activities You Enjoy Doing With Your Children

I remember the good old days when Jim and I used to play Ping-Pong. I used to beat him. But those days are gone forever. Now whenever we play, he beats me—really trounces me.

That isn't all. I used to beat him in bowling. But now he doesn't consider me much of a match.

And golf. I could drive a ball farther and putt straighter. But now he drives farther and putts straighter.

Through the years we have had a great time playing together. Now he has become the champ, and I'm proud of him!

Have you ever matched brains with your children in Scrabble? Have you taught them to golf? Be careful. Someday they will beat you!

Another activity they enjoy is going out for a Big Mac or to Burger King. When was the last time you took them, just for the fun of it?

Did you realize that going out for hamburgers and Cokes can be one of the most inexpensive times of counseling you can ever have with your children? It seems that while we're eating together away from the home situation, the children really open up and talk.

If going out like this is on your list of activities, you may have to watch your children. Mine pulled a trick on me. We went to Burger King. I asked what everybody wanted, and they all told me they wanted a Big Mac. I went to the counter and ordered Big Macs. The girl blinked, then smiled. "You get Big Macs at McDonald's," she told me.

I was so embarrassed. Then I turned around and saw that my children were all laughing. The joke was on me. They know more than you do about fast-food restaurants. So be on the lookout for their tricks.

But why not take them out for a hamburger and a Coke? As you sit there eating, you will be amazed at how they will open up and share with you what's on their minds. It really works.

Vacations could be on your list of activities. Personally I believe parents should take their children with them on vacations. We have had tremendous opportunities to share insights with our children as we have traveled together. It brought us great unity. Those times were—and in memory still are—very precious to Elsie and me.

Some family counselors recommend that the mother and father ought to get away by themselves at times. I agree—if it is just an overnight trip. But certainly if the vacation is going to be longer than that, you ought to take the children along with you.

This should give you an idea of the kinds of activities you can share with your children. Make a list of all the possibilities, and then start making them realities.

Third, Be Patient With Them

We parents easily forget all the mistakes we made when we were children.

What about the time you lied and didn't get caught? Or when you stole something from the corner store? Or played hookey from school?

Can you expect your children to be so different?

Children will make mistakes. That's part of growing up. After all, they are children. I have never yet met a perfect child, but I have met a number of imperfect children who were turned off by "perfect" parents!

When your children make mistakes, correct them—and then forget it. Don't keep bringing it up; that will make them rebellious. They know they have made a mistake, but your constant reminding them of that mistake will do more harm than good.

Act as though you have really forgotten it, and you have

taken care of the problem. Don't hold them off at arm's length.

When they are discouraged, encourage them. After all, remember how you feel when you are discouraged; that's the way they feel too. Isn't it a great feeling to have someone come along and help you out of the doldrums? We never forget a person who does that for us. Neither will your children.

So when they feel like giving up, encourage them to keep going. Those little boosts of inspiration will do a lot for them. Cite an example from your own life of how you once felt the same way but came out on top. That will also help to correct false images children sometimes have of their parents. They think parents are perfect. If we relate some of our failures, we will endear ourselves to them. They will see us as more "human." As we identify with their mistakes through the ones we have made, they will see us as more understanding and approachable.

Fourth, Share Bible Verses With Them

There is absolutely no substitute for the Scriptures in our Christian lives. As I said earlier, encourage your children to memorize and personalize the Scriptures.

For example, you are going through a trying time, and God makes a verse of the Bible especially real to you. Don't keep it to yourself. Share it with your children. Tell them how it relates to your present situation.

Be excited about the Scriptures, and let your children sense that excitement. If the Bible hasn't become exciting to you, because of your inability to experience it, then it will be difficult to get your children excited about it.

What do I mean by getting excited about Scripture?

Well, it is simply memorizing a Scripture verse and then seeing it work for you.

For instance, if you take a verse such as, "My God shall supply all your need according to his riches in glory by Christ Jesus" (Philippians 4:19), then have faith that God will indeed supply all your needs. Pick a specific need and apply that verse. Tell your children about it.

As you share the Scriptures, you share God's promises. When you believe those promises, you can't help but experience the results. One goes with the other. And that will make you excited about God's Word—because it is working in your life. When you get excited, your children will too.

Then it won't be long before they are coming to share Bible verses with you. Think of what that will mean during the times when you get discouraged! I have had a lot of moving experiences in my lifetime, but one that really thrills me is to have my children encourage me with the Scriptures.

Fifth, Help Them Plan for Their Futures

A friend of mine wanted more than anything else for his son to follow in his footsteps. Not wanting to disappoint his father, the boy studied business administration. After some frustrating years, he wanted to drop out of college. The father couldn't understand why, but finally it all came out. The son really wanted to be a minister but didn't pursue it, assuming his father would never understand.

But the father did understand. In fact, he was much more excited about his son's becoming a minister than a businessman. The son is now studying for the ministry, and both father and son are pleased and satisfied.

If you have more than one child, you have already discovered that no two children are ever exactly alike. It was my secret wish that our daughters would be like their mother and our son would be like me. But it won't happen that way. They are individuals—not carbon copies of us. We must accept the fact that God's plan for our children's lives may be quite different from His plan for our lives.

So encourage your children to seek God's guidance for their future. Then provide a listening ear for their ambitions and hopes in life. Pray with them for God's plan. And whatever that plan turns out to be, rejoice with them in it—it is God's plan. We have no better plan than His plan.

While your children are pursuing God's plan, be personally involved in whatever they would like to do. If they want to go to college, for example, help them secure the needed information to make their decision. Arrange for them to attend a "college day" on that campus, even if it means taking them. You need to see what that college is like too.

But suppose they go to college for a year and decide to quit. Be careful how you handle that. We have certain ideals for our children, but we have to be careful that we are not living their lives for them. They eventually have to learn to make their own decisions and live with the consequences of those decisions.

If they decide college isn't the way to go right now, encourage them to seek another path. Career analysts have told us it is healthy for young people to have varied backgrounds. Some try all sorts of things before they eventually get a sense of direction. The experience from many different jobs is to their benefit. Be careful about accusing them of not sticking to one thing long enough. They are probably gaining experience for future direction.

It is no fun for young people trying to make up their

minds about what they should do. To some it's overwhelming. Can you really feel the hurt they feel? Can you feel the confusion and frustration they feel? If you can, you are a real parent. If you can't, ask God to help you.

Here again, remember that each child is different. One will know from day one what he wants to do and follow right through with it. Another may seem as though he is taking forever to make up his mind. So don't try to put them all into the same mold. Don't unfairly compare one child with another.

When Elsie was a teenager, she wanted to take on a big responsibility, but she was discouraged at home from trying it. To this day she wishes she had been encouraged to use her musical talents as a witness at school.

If your child tells you he's going to be president of the United States, encourage him. He may not end up in the White House, but at least he knows you are behind him, that you believe in him.

Whatever your children want to do, don't try to convince them they are bound to fail at it. If they do fail, it may be more from your lack of faith in them than their lack of ability. So don't take that chance. Put your trust in them, and they will amaze you with their accomplishments.

Conclusion

Children are a "heritage of the Lord." He sends them into your home to bring joy in time of sorrow, help in time of need. They are indeed a blessing, not a curse.

So if you really want to enjoy your children, remember these suggestions:

1. Seek their advice. And don't put down every idea they offer.

2. Make a list of activities you enjoy doing with them. And follow through by doing those things.
3. Be patient with them; after all, they are children.
4. Share Bible verses with them, especially as you yourself get excited about living the Bible.
5. Help them plan their futures.

Children grow up in a hurry. Before you can turn around, they will be grown and gone. So if you haven't started doing it yet, you need to begin enjoying your children—right now!

16

How to Keep Your Children Out of Trouble

It is rare indeed that any parent will raise children without some trouble. Believe me, Elsie and I have had our moments with our children.

Many times I have heard a frantic mother and father say, "If we only knew how to keep our children out of trouble." Well, years of working with youth who have gotten into trouble leads me to offer these suggestions that may help you.

First, Know Where Your Children Are; Jesus Does

When a TV station in our area flashes across the screen every evening at ten o'clock, "Do you know where your children are?" tragically many parents don't know.

I read that a research firm decided to call some families at ten to ask parents if they knew where their children were. When the researchers called, they found that the children were at home; the parents were gone! Seventy-five percent of the children didn't know where their parents were! Perhaps someday I should write a sequel to this book and call it *Do You Know Where Your Parents Are?*

But back to the serious side. When your children are going out for the evening, be sure you know where they are going and when they will be getting back. If their plans do not meet with your approval, tell them they can't go.

But if you have to tell them they can't go, try to work out an alternative. Raising children requires compromises. If you think you are going to be dogmatic and win every point, you are going to be surprised. And you will be raising rebellious children.

Second, Never Give up on Your Children

I suppose one of the hardest tasks in our ministry is telling one of the girls that her parents no longer want her. That is devastating to a child.

It happened again recently. A little blonde had come to the end of her road. She had been passed around from foster parent to foster parent. Because of her problems, no one wanted her. And the poor dear was just twelve years old.

When she came to us, she was crying, and I just threw my arms around her and hugged her. She was so starved for affection that she hugged me tightly. I had to bite my tongue to keep my tears in check. No home. No parents. No one cared.

But we did. We were there to try to show her Christ's love and make up what she had lacked in life so far.

Can you imagine what a child feels like when he or she realizes that parents no longer care for them?

Now I know it's tough raising children. They aren't angels. That means your patience will be tried beyond the breaking point. You will be embarrassed to death. And you may come within a hair's breadth of a nervous breakdown. Yes, it's tough. I know that.

But don't give up on them. They won't be teenagers forever. Just hang in there, do your best, and let them know that you believe in them.

Suppose you do give up on them; then what happens? They won't straighten out. They'll be guided solely by their peers and those trying to drag them down.

Your children need you. They need your confidence in them to help guide them through their formative years.

Let me tell you something else. When you are older and they are older, they will respect and love you and take care of you. Why? Because you stuck by them when they needed you.

Third, Minimize Their Problems

I know that when young people get into trouble, it may seem as though your world has come to an end. The police may pull up to your house and come in and arrest them. They may be on drugs. They might have even committed murder. But let me tell you, it is not the end of the world.

Try the best you can to minimize their problems. By that, I'm not saying you should bury your head in the sand. I am merely suggesting that you try to look at them in perspective.

Problems have a way of killing motivation and the desire to live. But if we look at problems sensibly with our children, we will help them understand that these problems can become the stepping-stones to success.

Place the emphasis on doing right. Minimize doing wrong. Get them involved in worthwhile activities that will challenge their interests, aptitudes, and abilities.

In a previous chapter I discussed the importance of consistent punishment when they do wrong. They need that release from guilt. And what I am about to say is not contrary to that.

Some well-meaning parents think the end of the world has come when there is a problem in the family. Parents will say that the neighbors will never respect them again. Some parents even threaten to kill themselves because of the way their children are acting. Some threaten to have their children thrown into jail. They are making a bigger deal out of the situation than it warrants. Instead they ought to minimize their problems.

You see, everyone has problems. Sometimes people do a good job of hiding them. You might be amazed at what is really going on behind the walls of those houses down the block.

So don't be surprised when problems come to your home. It's a part of the price of being human. Let your children know that. But let them know there is a big difference between the Christian and the non-Christian. Both have problems. But the Christian can take his problems to the Lord and find the guidance that he needs to overcome. Let your children know that God is for us!

Fourth, Keep Them Active

I still believe that idleness is the devil's workshop. If your children are active in school and church, they won't have a lot of time to get into trouble.

Another help is to plan activities well ahead to give them something to look forward to. As soon as they get home from summer camp, start talking about next summer's camp. When you get back from your vacation, start planning your next vacation with them. Talk to them about their activities at school and church. Let them know you are happy with their being involved.

Being busy brings blessing. Busy young people have less time to think up ways of getting into trouble.

Help your children fill their days, weeks, months, and years with worthwhile activities. Of course, they must have adequate time for studies, sleep, and food. But help them fill in their other time slots because children who are active rarely get into serious problems.

I recommend you sit down with each child and plan an activity list that will challenge—but not frustrate—them.

Fifth, Keep Them Saved

What plans do you have right now to be sure your children maintain their Christian life?

Surprisingly many parents don't have the foggiest notion. They think that everything will take care of itself. But that usually doesn't happen. You must plan to make it happen.

Your child's activity list ought to include things he or she is doing with other young people from the church and in the church.

Some denominations have youth programs that send older teens to a foreign field for a month or so. There they catch a glimpse of real missionary work by participating in it. Some of the young people who have gone on these witnessing teams are themselves missionaries today. Look into that; see if it will help your children.

Living for Jesus is one way to keep your children out of trouble. When they stray from the straight and narrow, the Holy Spirit knows exactly how to bring great conviction on them, gently urging them back. What you could not do, the Holy Spirit can and will do. He will keep them.

Conclusion

God has a very special purpose for children. They are not meant to be trouble; they are meant to be a blessing in our homes.

If you want to keep your children out of trouble, then try these suggestions:

1. Know where they are and what they're doing.
2. Never give up on them.
3. Minimize their problems by getting them into perspective.
4. Keep them active and involved in worthwhile projects.
5. Provide for their spiritual stimulation.

Perhaps by now you are exhausted from all the recommendations I have shared with you. I hope so! That will mean you realize there is work to be done—and that you are already busily involved in helping your children!

God loves children. God loves your children. He is going to help them because He is more interested in their welfare than you are.

The Bible talks about our being "workers together with God." That goes for raising children too. What a privilege it is for us to work with Him and with the children He has entrusted to our care.

With His help, everything in your family is going to work out for your good and for your Heavenly Father's praise and glory. Believe it—and see it happen in your home too!